CORPORATE SUSTAINABILITY PLANNING ASSESSMENT GUIDE

CORPORATE SUSTAINABILITY PLANNING ASSESSMENT GUIDE

A Comprehensive Organizational Assessment

Donald C. Fisher, Ph.D.

ASQ Quality Press
Milwaukee, Wisconsin

American Society for Quality, Quality Press, Milwaukee 53203
© 2010 American Society for Quality
All rights reserved. Published 2009
Printed in the United States of America
13 12 11 10 09   5 4 3 2 1

Library of Congress Cataloging-in-Publication Data
Fisher, Donald C.
    Corporate sustainability planning assessment guide : a comprehensive organizational assessment /
    Donald C. Fisher.
        p. cm.
    Includes bibliographical references and indexes.
    ISBN 978-0-87389-774-7 (pbk. : alk. paper)
    1. Sustainable development. 2. Corporations—Environmental aspects. 3. Social responsibility of business.
    4. Economic development—Environmental aspects. I. Title.
    HC79.E5F524 2009
    658.4'012—dc22

                                                                                    2009023950

ISBN-13: 978-0-87389-774-7

Publisher: William A. Tony
Acquisitions Editor: Matt Meinholz
Project Editor: Paul O'Mara
Production Administrator: Randall Benson

ASQ Mission: The American Society for Quality advances individual, organizational, and community excellence worldwide through learning, quality improvement, and knowledge exchange.

Attention Bookstores, Wholesalers, Schools, and Corporations: ASQ Quality Press books, videotapes, audiotapes, and software are available at quantity discounts with bulk purchases for business, educational, or instructional use. For information, please contact ASQ Quality Press at 800-248-1946, or write to ASQ Quality Press, P.O. Box 3005, Milwaukee, WI 53201-3005.

To place orders or to request a free copy of the ASQ Quality Press Publications Catalog, including ASQ membership information, call 800-248-1946. Visit our Web site at http://www.asq.org or http://www.asq.org/quality-press

∞ Printed on acid-free paper

Quality Press
600 N. Plankinton Avenue
Milwaukee, Wisconsin 53203
Call toll free 800-248-1946
Fax 414-272-1734
www.asq.org
http://www.asq.org/quality-press
http://standardsgroup.asq.org
E-mail: authors@asq.org

ASQ
AMERICAN SOCIETY
FOR QUALITY®

This book is dedicated to my grandchildren,
Marissa Jae Moore and Landon Cole Moore,
who will ensure sustainability for future
generations within our family.

Contents

CD-ROM Contents

Organizational Overview
Category 1: Leadership
Category 2: Strategic Planning
Category 3: Customer Focus
Category 4: Measurement, Analysis, and Knowledge Management
Category 5: Workforce Focus
Category 6: Process Management
Category 7: Results
Corporate Sustainability Score Sheet
Hierarchy of Corporate Sustainability Assessment Needs
Transformation of Assessment Findings
Strategic Planning Worksheet
Quick and Easy Supplier/Customer Assessment for Corporate Sustainability
Corporate Sustainability Benchmarking Process
Checklist for 100 Corporate Sustainability Considerations to Benchmark
Corporate Sustainability Documentation List
Corporate Sustainability Assessment Interview Plan and Timetable
Corporate Green Sustainability Index (CGSI)
Global Reporting Initiative (GRI) Index
Suggested Corporate Sustainability Report Outline
Corporate Sustainability Report Planning Worksheets
Corporate Sustainability Plan and Budget

Foreword

Imagine if your organization was able to balance environmental, economic, and social sustainability as part of a larger strategic plan. With *Corporate Sustainability Planning Assessment Manual: A Comprehensive Organizational Assessment*, Donald C. Fisher, PhD., has applied his vast knowledge of organizational improvement to sustainability. The result of that effort is a valuable tool that will help your organization integrate sustainability principles into its broader vision.

Dr. Fisher has been helping organizations improve quality for more than 20 years. His background and experience with Malcolm Baldrige Award Criteria, and how to best help organizations comply with that criteria, give him a unique perspective from which we can all learn and improve.

In my own organization, Methodist Le Bonheur Healthcare (MLH), we're applying Dr. Fisher's assessment tools as we pursue our own sustainability efforts. We believe stewardship of the earth's resources is consistent with our mission, vision, and values. Our responsibility in the community extends far beyond just meeting today's healthcare needs. With the tools in Dr. Fisher's book, MLH can better plan and execute purposefully for the future, to ensure the ongoing health of our Associates, our patients, and our community. That's the true focus of sustainability.

Whether your organization is just beginning its journey, or leading the way to a sustainable future, Dr. Fisher's *Corporate Sustainability Planning Assessment Manual* can help you achieve your strategic business goals and help your organization lay a foundation built upon the principles of sustainability.

Gary S. Shorb
President and Chief Executive Officer
Methodist Le Bonheur Healthcare

Preface

The concept and scope of sustainability efforts entail the integration of economic, environmental, and social issues that an organization impacts. The most common definition of sustainability was created in 1987 by the Brundtland Commission, formally the World Commission on Environment and Development (WCED). It noted that sustainability does not focus solely on environmental issues, but on three foundations of economic growth: economic, environmental, and social factors.

Corporate sustainability planning has risen in prominence over the past few years among leading organizations as a tool to achieve strategic dominance within the global marketplace. Organizational sustainability is being addressed in both the Dow Jones Sustainability Group Indexes and the Global 100 Most Sustainable Corporations in the World initiative that was launched in 2005 and presented annually at the World Economic Forum in Davos, Switzerland.

The Dow Jones Sustainability Group Indexes were developed to meet the financial markets' demands for an investment index to benchmark over 200 organizations committed to sustainable business practices. The Indexes recognize how organizations integrate economic, environmental, and social factors into their business strategies. The Indexes place particular emphasis on innovative technology, corporate governance, stakeholder interests, industry leadership, and corporate responses to societal changes. The Indexes are reviewed annually by an advisory committee that consists of experts from both the financial and corporate sustainability sectors.

The Global 100 Most Sustainable Corporations in the World project addresses corporate sustainability. The Global 100 list of publicly-traded, world-listed companies are assessed on how they manage sustainability regarding environmental, social, and governance (ESG) risks and opportunities.

Corporate sustainability planning for an organization builds on its core values, and can provide direction and rationale for the integration of sustainability principles among employees, vendors, and customers. This comprehensive manual will aid an organization in identifying strategic opportunities for improvement regarding their sustainability efforts. The manual will be most valuable in developing and/or improving a corporate sustainability plan, and will help an organization identify and strategically address sustainability opportunities that will:

- Increase revenue and reduce costs
- Enhance the organization's reputation, brand, and market value
- Better attract and retain talented employees
- Mitigate regulatory and business risks
- Address key economic, environmental, and social issues within the organization

Introduction

The globally integrated economy of the 21st century is providing new opportunities and spawning new kinds of dynamics and challenges. These call for innovation in management systems, workforce models, employee engagement, corporate policy changes, and stakeholder diversity that require organizations to apply new methodologies to ensure ongoing corporate sustainability.

Corporate Sustainability Planning

Corporate sustainability planning for an organization balances the need for economic growth with environmental protection and social equality. It is an evolving concept that organizational leaders are adopting because it makes good business sense. Reducing waste and inefficiency within an organization can save money and protect the environment. Systems-based pollution protection and sound environmental management can be good for employees, customers, and vendors. Organizations derive through strategic sustainability planning an alignment of business objectives such as profit and competitiveness with sound economic, environmental, and social principles in place. Sustainability Planning presents strategies for organizations to generate profits and save costs while contributing to the well-being of the planet and its people.[1]

The concept of corporate sustainability planning provides an enlightened and disciplined management approach of corporate resources throughout an organization.

Sustainability—A New Management Philosophy

Corporate sustainability can be viewed as a new and evolving management philosophy that addresses organizational growth and profitability, environmental protection, social justice, and equality (economic/environmental/social).

Sustainability is referenced by environmentalists as *ecological sustainability* and by many in the business community as *economic sustainability*, whereas sociologists reference it as "social sustainability."[2] Corporate sustainability efforts therefore promote the integration and balance of all three sustainability concepts. They ensure sustainability in corporate service and/or product developments and offerings for future generations of employees, customers, and stakeholder groups.

Several recurrent themes regarding corporate sustainability are addressed throughout this manual. These include:

- Management of organizational growth by polluting the environment less
- Development of processes that ensure sustainability in key products and/or service offerings throughout the organization
- Development of governance and leadership philosophies that promote sustainability throughout the organization, and among key supplier and customer networks that are aligned with the organization
- Development of corporate policies and procedures, partnerships, top leadership commitment, and involvement with various stakeholder groups
- Addressing financial viability and key economic, environmental, and social issues
- Meeting the corporate needs of the present leadership without compromising the ability of future generations of corporate leaders to ensure stability within the organization regarding economic, environmental, and societal issues
- Ensuring that diversity is being considered in all corporate hiring, training, and employee development programs and offerings

- Ensuring that human rights are being considered before securing services and/or products from various vendor groups
- Developing strategic short- and longer-term planning initiatives that promote corporate sustainability
- Consideration of environmental impacts on all new service and product offerings
- Addressing and attempting to resolve employee, customer, supplier, and stakeholder concerns that relate to economic, environmental, and societal issues
- Evaluation of risk management and regulatory initiatives that are in place to help ensure corporate sustainability
- Recognition of employees, vendors, and customers who exhibit notable sustainability practices
- Documentation of key sustainability practices and/or processes throughout the organization[3]

Sustainability Issues and Strategic Opportunities

Organizations face a wide array of sustainability issues today. Many small and mid-sized organizations lack a holistic strategic plan to address them or have a piecemeal and uncoordinated plan in place. The lack of a coordinated plan may result in the organization being exposed to unnecessary business risks and missing out on strategic opportunities for future growth and development.[4]

Corporate sustainability planning incorporates a wide array of diverse areas, which includes organizational issues such as business strategy, leadership and management development, finance, environmental issues, ethics, management of human resources, diversity, industry and community issues, health and safety, corporate governance, and labor relations.[5]

In order for an organization to strategically address this large array of sustainability issues and to help achieve its vision and mission, the use of the Malcolm Baldrige Criteria for Performance Excellence has been incorporated throughout this manual as an assessment tool.

Global Sustainability Indexes and Criteria

There are many global criteria for sustainability that are used by organizations and profit-seeking investors, such as the Dow Jones Sustainability Indexes, The Ethibel Sustainability Index, Ethical Global Index, FTSE4Good Global 100 Index, Humanix 200 Global, Ethinvest Environmental Index Australia, Jantzi Social Index Canada, Johannesburg Stock Exchange/FTSE4Good Index South Africa, and the Humanix 50 Index Sweden. Many of the indices' criteria are related, but are written with specific emphasis on various sustainability issues. In many cases the various criteria appear vague for organizations to use in developing their corporate sustainability plans.[6]

The various index criteria appear to be theoretical, and difficult to understand and simplify to support a strategic focus and a holistic view of an organization's overall sustainable initiatives and strategic opportunities for future implementation. The most notable existing model that is being used by various industries both in the United States and globally is the Criteria for Performance Excellence from the Baldrige National Quality Award Program that was developed in the United States. This model has indices in place that are aligned with several of the global sustainability indexes presently in place. The Baldrige Criteria not only promotes sustainability efforts, but provides a framework to identify and implement sustainability initiatives that can be strategically aligned and used to promote performance excellence throughout an organization.[7]

About This Manual

This manual can be used to conduct a comprehensive organizational assessment based on Performance Excellence Criteria. These guidelines for evaluating or revising an existing corporate sustainability plan and/or developing a new plan can provide a unique perspective regarding various vulnerabilities that exist within an organization's overall infrastructure.

1 How to Assess Your Organization for Corporate Sustainability Planning

The alignment of the Performance Excellence Criteria with Corporate Sustainability Planning provides a unique assessment methodology for an organization to gauge its corporate sustainability planning efforts. The Baldrige Criteria for Performance Excellence have been recognized as a "best practice" initiative for organizations to use to assess and to ensure that their sustainability performance is competitive in the global marketplace.

An organization would want to assess itself using the Performance Excellence Criteria because thousands of U.S. organizations stay abreast of ever-increasing competition and improve their overall performance using this internationally recognized quality standard. The Criteria can help an organization align resources and approaches, and improve corporate-wide communications, productivity, and effectiveness regarding sustainability planning efforts.

The Corporate Sustainability assessment scoring system is based on two evaluation dimensions: (1) process and (2) results. Each dimension should be considered before assigning a percentage score. All process evaluation dimension categories are linked to results, as well as being linked to each other. In addition, each of the categories assessed will have Corporate Sustainability Scoring Profiles based on Corporate Sustainability Progression issues.

Process Evaluation Dimension (Categories 1–6)

Process refers to the methods your organization uses and improves to address the item requirements in Categories 1-6. The four factors used to evaluate process are approach, deployment, learning, and integration (A-D-L-I).

Approach (A) refers to:

- The methods used to accomplish the process
- The appropriateness of the methods to the item requirements
- The effectiveness of use of the methods
- The degree to which the approach is repeatable and based on reliable data and information (that is, systematic)

Deployment (D) refers to the extent to which:

- The approach is applied in addressing item requirements relevant and important to your organization
- The approach is applied consistently
- The approach is used by all appropriate work units

Learning (L) refers to:

- The refining of your approach through cycles of evaluation and improvement
- The encouraging of breakthrough change to your approach through innovation
- The sharing of refinements and innovation with other relevant work units and processes in your organization

1

Integration (I) refers to the extent to which:

- The approach is aligned with your organizational needs identified in other criteria item requirements
- The measures, information, and improvement systems are complementary across processes and work units
- The plans, processes, results, analysis, learning, and actions are harmonized across processes and work units to support organization-wide goals[8]

Results Evaluation Dimension (Category 7)

Results refers to your organization's outputs and outcomes in achieving the requirements in items 7.1-7.6. The five factors used to evaluate results are performance levels, trends, comparisons, linkage, and gap (Le-T-C-Li-G). *Performance Levels* (Le) refers to:

- Performance position of data
- Rank of data performance
- Current data performance
- Numerical information that places or positions the organization's results and performance on a meaningful measurement scale

Trends (T) refers to:

- Ratio (that is, slope of trend data)
- Breadth (that is, how widely deployed and shared)

Comparisons (C) refers to:

- Performance relative to appropriate comparisons
- Comparisons against exemplary results

Linkage (Li) refers to:

- Alignment of data to important customer product and service, process, and action plan performance requirements
- Complementary measures and results that are aligned throughout many parts of the organization
- Connective measures throughout the organization that drive key organizational strategies and goals

Gap (G) refers to:

- An interval in results data
- Missing segments of data[9]

Importance as a Scoring Consideration

The two evaluation dimensions, described in the previous sections, are critical to evaluation and feedback. However, another critical consideration in evaluation and feedback is the importance of your reported process and results to your organization's key business factors (that is, key customer requirements, competitive environment, key strategic objectives, and action plans).[10]

The percent scores range from a low of 0 percent for zero-based preparation to a high of 100 percent for world-class preparation. An organization can be 0 percent (zero-based) in some areas and 100 percent (world-class) in others. The anchor point is 50 percent, which is middle range. Many organizations fall below the 50 percent anchor point regarding Corporate Sustainability Planning. The 50 percent anchor point is considered to be good, but certainly below what an organization that is striving to be the "best-in-class" in sustainability preparation and progression among leading organizations would score.

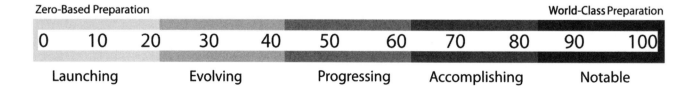

Zero-Based Preparation   World-Class Preparation

| 0 | 10 | 20 | 30 | 40 | 50 | 60 | 70 | 80 | 90 | 100 |

Launching   Evolving   Progressing   Accomplishing   Notable

Organizations that score 0 percent have an anecdotal approach, lack deployment, and have no meaningful sustainability results. Organizations that score 100 percent reflect a refined, very mature approach that is deployed and well adapted with sustainable results in all relevant areas of the organization.

Scoring Profiles Based on Corporate Sustainability Progression Levels

Scoring profiles based on the Corporate Sustainability Planning progression levels are provided in this manual to aid the team's scoring process. The teams should first consider the two dimensions (Process and Results) and review the Corporate Sustainability Scoring Profile section. The scoring profiles will aid the team in further profiling and fine-tuning the percentile range in which the scores should fall.

Sustainability Levels of Progression

1. **Launching (0-20 percent)**   The organization is beginning to initiate its sustainability efforts corporate-wide. Leaders do not fully promote corporate sustainability efforts, nor holistically understand how they can be aligned with the organization's strategic planning process.
2. **Evolving (20-40 percent)**   The organization is implementing sustainability efforts in some departments/divisions corporate-wide. Senior leaders are beginning to support corporate-wide sustainability and are reviewing the inclusion of a few sustainability efforts within the organization's strategic planning process.
3. **Progressing (40-60 percent)**   The organization's senior leadership is committed to sustainability and has a well-defined plan to deploy their strategic efforts throughout the workforce. Customer/supplier/employee support systems are in place to ensure ongoing sustainability efforts are being initiated and managed throughout the organization. A corporate sustainability plan is being developed and aligned with the organization's strategic planning efforts.
4. **Accomplishing (60-80 percent)**   The organization's senior leaders promote sustainability efforts among the workforce, suppliers, and customer groups. A corporate sustainability plan has been developed and aligned with the organization's strategic plan. Managers, employees, suppliers, and customers are rewarded/recognized for their involvement in promoting corporate sustainability efforts and for helping the organization achieve sustainable results internally, throughout the community, and within the industry.
5. **Notable (80-100 percent)**   The organization's senior leadership is visibly involved in promoting corporate sustainability efforts to employees, suppliers, customers, and the community where the organization conducts business. The organization has become a community and industry model for its sustainability efforts and has become a global benchmark for corporate sustainability practices. The organization's sustainability practices are well-documented with results that have positive three to five year trends.

Corporate Sustainability Scoring Profiles
1. Leadership

Sustainability Levels of Progression	World-Class Preparation	
	Notable 80-100%	• Senior leadership is visibly involved in promoting corporate sustainability industry-wide. • Senior leaders promote the formation of employee teams throughout the organization to focus on corporate sustainability issues corporate-wide. • Senior leadership reflects the organization's commitment to environmental and societal sustainability issues corporate-wide.
	Accomplishing 60-80%	• Most senior leaders promote corporate sustainability initiatives among employees. • Senior leadership meets with employee teams, key suppliers, partners, and customers on corporate sustainability issues. • Leadership at all levels promotes corporate sustainability as a major priority for the organization.
	Progressing 40-60%	• Senior leadership shares corporate values regarding corporate sustainability priorities with employees, customers, partners, and suppliers. • Senior leadership is committed to public responsibility and corporate leadership regarding corporate sustainability. • Senior leaders support short- and long-term strategic planning for corporate sustainability.
	Evolving 20-40%	• A few senior leaders and managers support and are involved in the organization's corporate sustainability efforts. • Corporate sustainability initiatives exist in some parts of the organization. • The organization's corporate policies and procedures reflect some commitment to corporate sustainability.
	Launching 0-20%	• Some leaders are beginning to support organizational involvement in corporate sustainability initiatives. • Senior leadership is beginning to get involved with employees, suppliers, partners, and customers regarding corporate sustainability issues and concerns. • Senior leadership has a limited corporate sustainability plan in place.
	Zero-Based Preparation	

Process Dimension (Categories 1-6)
Evaluation Factors

☑   **Approach** (methods used to accomplish the process)

☑   **Deployment** (application of the approach throughout the organization)

☑   **Learning** (refinement of the approach through cycles of evaluation)

☑   **Integration** (alignment of the approach throughout the organization)

Corporate Sustainability Scoring Profiles
2. Strategic Planning

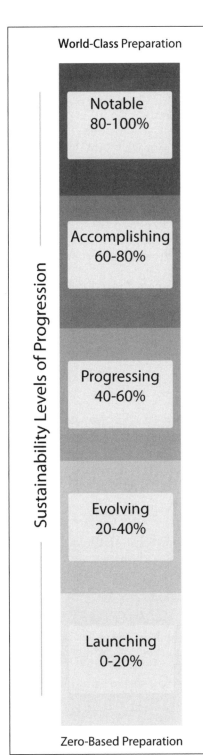

World-Class Preparation	
Notable 80-100%	• The organization's strategic planning process includes corporate sustainability initiatives. • The organization seeks and receives corporate sustainability input from employees, suppliers, partners, and customers before developing a strategic plan. • The strategic planning process for corporate sustainability includes short- and longer-term plans based on key data, customer, supplier, partner, and employee survey data, and benchmark data deployed throughout the organization.
Accomplishing 60-80%	• Senior management provides corporate sustainability input and approves the alignment of the corporate sustainability plan with the organization's strategic planning process. • Operational corporate sustainability plans linked to the master strategic plan are developed throughout the organization. • Managers are held accountable for meeting strategic corporate sustainability goals and objectives.
Progressing 40-60%	• Operational corporate sustainability plans developed at department levels link with master plan. • The organization involves employees, suppliers, partners, and customers in corporate sustainability planning process. • Managers at all levels are held accountable for meeting corporate sustainability goals and objectives.
Evolving 20-40%	• Strategic corporate sustainability goals are established for key functional areas of the organization. • Some employees, suppliers, partners, and customers are involved in the corporate sustainability strategic planning. • Some senior managers are involved in corporate sustainability planning.
Launching 0-20%	• A few employees, suppliers, partners, and customers are involved in planning for corporate sustainability. • Corporate sustainability planning is being reviewed for inclusion in the organization's strategic planning process. • Employees beyond senior managers are beginning to be involved in planning for corporate sustainability initiatives.
Zero-Based Preparation	

Sustainability Levels of Progression

Process Dimension (Categories 1-6)
Evaluation Factors

☑ **Approach** (methods used to accomplish the process)

☑ **Deployment** (application of the approach throughout the organization)

☑ **Learning** (refinement of the approach through cycles of evaluation)

☑ **Integration** (alignment of the approach throughout the organization)

Corporate Sustainability Scoring Profiles
3. Customer Focus

Sustainability Levels of Progression	
World-Class Preparation	
Notable 80-100%	• The organization conducts surveys, focus groups, and exit interviews to determine customer requirements for corporate sustainability. • The organization promotes trust and confidence in its products/services to customers regarding corporate sustainability. • The organization is continuously gauging customer and market requirements and expectations regarding corporate sustainability.
Accomplishing 60-80%	• Effective feedback systems are in place to obtain critical customer and market data regarding corporate sustainability. • Customer contact employees are given corporate sustainability training. • Logistical support is in place for customers to receive corporate sustainability support.
Progressing 40-60%	• Effective customer support regarding corporate sustainability is in place. • A complaint management process for customer concerns regarding corporate sustainability is in place. • Customer-contact employees are trained on corporate sustainability issues.
Evolving 20-40%	• Some customer groups and markets are segmented regarding corporate sustainability requirements. • Customer follow-up system is being developed to address corporate sustainability issues. • Future corporate sustainability expectations and requirements are determined and considered for future implementation among many customers.
Launching 0-20%	• Organization is beginning to promote trust and confidence with customers regarding corporate sustainability issues. • Organization surveys its customers/markets regarding corporate sustainability issues. • Organization is beginning to consider corporate sustainability a customer service issue.
Zero-Based Preparation	

Process Dimension (Categories 1-6)
Evaluation Factors

☑ **Approach** (methods used to accomplish the process)
☑ **Deployment** (application of the approach throughout the organization)
☑ **Learning** (refinement of the approach through cycles of evaluation)
☑ **Integration** (alignment of the approach throughout the organization)

Corporate Sustainability Scoring Profiles
4. Measurement, Analysis, and Knowledge Management

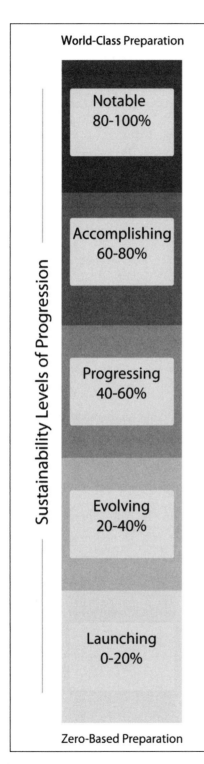

World-Class Preparation

Notable
80-100%

- Processes and technology to ensure timely, accurate, valid, and useful corporate sustainability data for employees, suppliers, partners, and customers is in place.
- Competitive comparisons and benchmarking information and data are used to improve and maintain corporate sustainability.
- Corporate sustainability data is analyzed organization-wide by employee teams that translate it into useful information to help sustain the workplace environment..

Accomplishing
60-80%

- Employees have rapid access to corporate sustainability data throughout the organization.
- Comparative corporate sustainability data is collected, analyzed, and translated into useful information to support a secure workplace.
- Processes and technologies are used across most of the organization to ensure that corporate sustainability data is complete, timely, accurate, valid, and useful.

Progressing
40-60%

- Employees have access to corporate sustainability data in many parts of the organization.
- Most critical processes have corporate sustainability data that is complete, accurate, and timely.
- Measures exist that gauge corporate sustainability effectiveness throughout the organization.

Evolving
20-40%

- Corporate sustainability data exist for some critical products/ services and processes.
- Organization ensures that hardware and software are reliable, secure, and user-friendly regarding corporate sustainability.
- Corporate sustainability data and knowledge is transferred to key customers, suppliers, and partners.

Launching
0-20%

- Corporate sustainability data received for comparison is beginning to be collected.
- Limited corporate sustainability data is used to ensure a sustainable workplace for employees.
- Collection of corporate sustainability data is in the beginning stages within the organization and is being shared with some customers, suppliers, and partners.

Zero-Based Preparation

Sustainability Levels of Progression

Process Dimension (Categories 1-6)
Evaluation Factors

☑ **Approach** (methods used to accomplish the process)

☑ **Deployment** (application of the approach throughout the organization)

☑ **Learning** (refinement of the approach through cycles of evaluation)

☑ **Integration** (alignment of the approach throughout the organization)

Corporate Sustainability Scoring Profiles
5. Workforce Focus

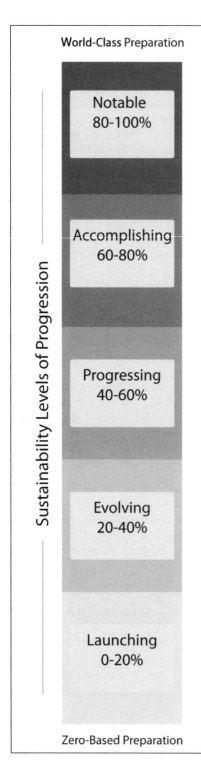

World-Class Preparation

Notable
80-100%

- The organization is highly sensitive to employee well-being and satisfaction regarding corporate sustainability.
- Organization supports corporate sustainability plans and goals through employee education, training, and development initiatives.
- Organization supports workplace sustainability by promoting cross-functional teams to address and to be recognized for innovative problem-solving approaches in identifying and resolving corporate sustainability issues.

Accomplishing
60-80%

- Senior and middle management support and recognize employee involvement, contributions, and teamwork in resolving corporate sustainability issues.
- Employee idea sharing and innovation is encouraged regarding corporate sustainability.
- Employees are empowered and rewarded when they identify and address corporate sustainability issues.

Progressing
40-60%

- Corporate sustainability awareness is promoted within many parts of the organization.
- Employees are given corporate sustainability training on an annual basis.
- Management supports cross-functional teams to identify corporate sustainability opportunities for the organization.

Evolving
20-40%

- Managers in some parts of the organization support employee involvement in corporate sustainability.
- Organization keeps employees informed regarding corporate sustainability issues in some management meetings.
- Employee training initiatives address some corporate sustainability issues.

Launching
0-20%

- Few employees within the organization are empowered to work on corporate sustainability issues.
- Workforce is periodically surveyed regarding its well-being and satisfaction with the organization's corporate sustainability initiatives.
- Employees involved with improving corporate sustainability are periodically recognized by the organization.

Zero-Based Preparation

Sustainability Levels of Progression

Process Dimension (Categories 1-6)
Evaluation Factors

☑ **Approach** (methods used to accomplish the process)

☑ **Deployment** (application of the approach throughout the organization)

☑ **Learning** (refinement of the approach through cycles of evaluation)

☑ **Integration** (alignment of the approach throughout the organization)

Corporate Sustainability Scoring Profiles
6. Process Management

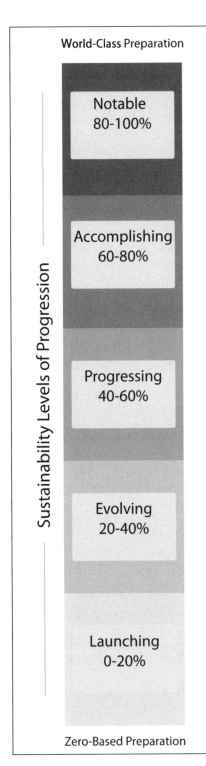

World-Class Preparation

Sustainability Levels of Progression

Notable
80-100%

- Key corporate sustainability processes have been identified and documented across the organization.
- Systematic approaches are used to document corporate sustainability processes to ensure shortened cycle time and consistent procedures.
- Critical corporate sustainability processes are reviewed on an on-going basis to reduce variability, and to keep the processes current with sustainability needs and directions.

Accomplishing
60-80%

- Key corporate sustainability processes are documented and controlled across the organization.
- Comprehensive corporate sustainability assessments are conducted throughout the organization on an annual basis.
- Analytic problem-solving tools are used within the organization to improve corporate sustainability processes.

Progressing
40-60%

- Process assessments are conducted in many parts of the organization to ensure key corporate sustainability issues have been identified, documented, and flowcharted.
- Customer, supplier, partner, and employee input are used to flowchart and document key processes identified for corporate sustainability.
- Organization identifies and documents key processes which support corporate sustainability.

Evolving
20-40%

- Corporate sustainability assessments are conducted only when key customers complain.
- Not all critical corporate sustainability issues have been identified and addressed.
- Limited customer, supplier, and partner input is incorporated into documentation of corporate sustainability designs.

Launching
0-20%

- Organization is beginning to identify and document key corporate sustainability issues regarding its assessment of corporate sustainability issues.
- Some corporate sustainability assessments are conducted.
- Corporate sustainability issues to ensure a safe work environment are beginning to be addressed and documented.

Zero-Based Preparation

Process Dimension (Categories 1-6)
Evaluation Factors

☑ **Approach** (methods used to accomplish the process)
☑ **Deployment** (application of the approach throughout the organization)
☑ **Learning** (refinement of the approach through cycles of evaluation)
☑ **Integration** (alignment of the approach throughout the organization)

Corporate Sustainability Scoring Profiles
7. Results

Sustainability Levels of Progression	
World-Class Preparation	
Notable 80-100%	• Customer satisfaction results regarding corporate sustainability have shown positive results over the past three years. • Corporate sustainability performance results have experienced a steady improvement over the past five years. • Employee suggestions for corporate sustainability improvement and innovative sustainable work practices show positive trends over the past several years.
Accomplishing 60-80%	• The organization's corporate sustainability improvement results reflect improvement in cycle time and operational performance. • Key measures of the organization's corporate sustainability reflect cycle time reductions, and cost results have improved over the past three years in most parts of the organization. • Comparative corporate sustainability benchmark results reveal that the organization is leadings its industry.
Progressing 40-60%	• Key measures of corporate sustainability within Operations, Shipping, and Customer Contact reflects a three-year trend of positive results. • Supplier partnerships with the organization's corporate sustainability efforts show positive trends over the past three years. • Customer involvement with corporate sustainability issues reflects positive results over the past two years.
Evolving 20-40%	• Customer satisfaction with corporate sustainability shows positive results and trends. • Employee involvement in corporate sustainability projects has shown positive results over the past two years. • Employee satisfaction with the organization's corporate sustainability efforts shows positive trends over the past three years.
Launching 0-20%	• A few corporate sustainability benchmark results are collected by the organization. • Employee satisfaction with corporate sustainability issues within the organization is surveyed and results used to better identify sustainability issues. • The organization is beginning to use data to identify key corporate sustainability issues that are important to customers.
Zero-Based Preparation	

Results Dimension (Categories 7)
Evaluation Factors

☑   **Performance Levels** (position of data performance)
☑   **Trends** (rate and breadth of data)
☑   **Comparisons** (results relative to appropriate benchmarks)
☑   **Linkage** (alignment of data with key organizational initiatives)
☑   **Gap** (missing segments of data)

2 How to Use the Manual

How to Use the Corporate Sustainability Manual

This manual is designed to serve as an easy-to-use guide for an organization's cross-functional self-assessment team(s) to assess and score its corporate sustainability efforts.

This manual can be used to provide a due diligence for an organization's corporate sustainability efforts, and to provide a template for its self-assessment and strategic planning of corporate sustainability efforts. In addition, the manual provides guidance for employees and employee teams to score their departments or total organization in many areas, and serves as an annual benchmark for corporate sustainability improvement and a strategic guide for short-term and longer-term corporate sustainability planning. The manual assists employees in determining their organization's sustainability readiness. The manual can also be used to help employees collect sustainability data to benchmark against other *best practice* organizations and to ultimately develop a corporate sustainability plan.

How to Begin and Prepare for an Assessment

The assessment of an organization should begin with the full support and sponsorship of the senior leadership. The senior leadership should appoint a corporate sustainability assessment team administrator.

The first step in preparing for the assessment should include conducting a corporate sustainability assessment briefing for senior leadership. This session can be conducted by the organization's Chief Sustainability Officer (CSO) or the person who has been selected by senior leadership. The staff member appointed to conduct the briefing should review this manual and have a thorough understanding of sustainability issues before conducting the session.

In addition, senior leadership must be educated in sustainability issues to appreciate the value of conducting the assessment. Activities recommended to help senior leaders develop an understanding include the following:

- Reading books and articles on corporate sustainability issues (a suggested resource list is included in this manual on page 237)
- Benchmarking other public/private organizations to review best practices (see Appendix B)
- Completing the Corporate Green Sustainability Index (see Appendix F)

After senior leaders have been briefed, the assessment team administrator should begin the process of soliciting assessment team members. Many organizations solicit members through their corporate newsletter, email, or a personal letter sent from the President/CEO inviting participation. Team members' selections should be considered from a group of employees who have expressed an interest in better understanding and improving their organization's corporate sustainability infrastructure.

Once team members have been selected, it is recommended that an assessment workshop be conducted by the assessment team administrator or team participants who have an understanding of corporate sustainability. The workshop may include using a case study for the team to practice identifying organizational strengths and opportunities for corporate sustainability improvement in at least one or two categories. During the workshop, the team will discuss each category and determine "What does this mean for my organization?" The use of this manual will help the team practice translating corporate sustainability issues into simple language for their own organization-wide assessment.

Assessing the Organization

Team Member Selection

Assessment team members should represent a cross-section of employees. All departments throughout the organization should be represented on the teams. Diversity adds value and strength to each assessment team.

In larger organizations, seven corporate sustainability assessment category sub-teams would need to be developed. A subject matter expert (SME) for a particular category should be elected as the category team leader. In smaller organizations where there are a limited number of personnel who could serve on assessment teams, all categories can be assessed by one team. Following are some sample assessment team compositions:

ASSESSMENT TEAM COMPOSITION (LARGE ORGANIZATION) (20 to 50 MEMBERS)

Team 1: Leadership

CEO, President, or Senior VP (Team Leader)
Chief Sustainability Officer (CSO)
Director of Legal
Director of Public Policy
Manager of Operations
Customer
Supplier
Partner

Team 2: Strategic Planning

VP, Strategic Planning (Team Leader)
Chief Sustainability Officer (CSO)
Director
Manager
Supervisor
Customer
Supplier
Partner

Team 3: Customer Focus

VP, Marketing (Team Leader)
Director
Manager
Supervisor
Customer
Supplier
Partner

Team 4: Measurement, Analysis and Knowledge Management

VP, IT (Team Leader)
Director of IT
Manager
Supervisor
Customer
Supplier
Partner

Team 5: Workforce Focus

VP, Human Resources (Team Leader)
Director
Manager
Supervisor
Customer
Supplier
Partner

Team 6: Process Management

VP, Operations (Team Leader)
Director
Manager
Supervisor
Customer
Supplier
Partner

Team 7: Results

VP, Strategic Planning (Team Leader)
Director
Manager
Supervisor
Customer
Supplier
Partner

Note: Some teams may decide to assess only selected categories within their organization that appear weak in deploying corporate sustainability initiatives. This manual allows for complete flexibility regarding the extent to which an organization conducts its assessment.

ASSESSMENT TEAM COMPOSITION (SMALL ORGANIZATION)
(6 to 8 Members)

Team Assesses All Seven Sustainability Categories
- President/CEO or Senior VP (Team Leader)
- Chief Sustainability Officer (CSO)
- Director
- Manager
- Supervisor
- Customer
- Supplier/Partner

Pre-Assessment Meeting for Each Team
Sustainability Category team(s) will need to hold a pre-assessment planning meeting to identify individuals to be interviewed during the assessment. Dates and interview times need to be agreed upon during this session, and an agenda and timetable should be prepared. After the team selects the individuals within the organization to be interviewed, a team leader needs to contact all persons to be interviewed.

Coordination of Assessment Team Schedules
The assessment team administrator should coordinate all seven Category team schedules with Sustainability Category team leaders, and develop an overall assessment interview plan and timetable (see Appendix D). This schedule and timetable should then be submitted to the senior leadership of the organization for review and approval.

Team Interview of Selected Participants
After approval has been secured from senior leadership, each team is ready to begin its interview process with selected participants. The entire category team(s) will take turns interviewing the participants. This allows for more interaction and input for the assessment team. During the interview process, all assessment team members will have a copy of this manual in hand and will make notes under each of the questions. Each category team may choose to interview two to three groups of participants representing various levels throughout the organization. Interviewing hints and tips are provided in Appendix D. A corporate sustainability documentation list form is provided in Appendix E for the team(s) to use to list documents used to validate participant responses to the interview questions.

Assessment Team Consensus and Scoring of the Category
After all category interviews have been completed, the category team leaders will hold a consensus review meeting in which all team members will review the findings regarding areas identified as strengths and opportunities for improvement. The team will assign each item a percentile score and will ultimately award the category a total point score. A quick and easy organizational assessment for the organization's suppliers, partners, and customers is provided (see Appendix A) to help determine to what extent supplier and customer organizations have approached and deployed corporate sustainability initiatives within their own organizations. This quick assessment may also be used as a preliminary analysis of one's own organization or to benchmark another organization's corporate sustainability progress.

Entire Assessment Report Consolidated and Delivered
All seven Sustainability Category teams will deliver their assessment to the assessment team administrator. The assessment team administrator will meet with all category team leaders to review results. After the assessment team administrator and all seven category team leaders have reached a consensus on the strengths, opportunities for improvement, corporate sustainability planning issues (economic, environmental, and social), category percentile scores, and the overall assessment point score, the assessment is finalized and a corporate sustainability plan can be developed (see Chapter 10). The completed assessment and corporate sustainability plan is then delivered to the President/CEO and the other senior staff members. The entire assessment process can take as little as two weeks or as much as one month to complete.

Organizational Overview
(Complete before conducting corporate sustainability assessment)

Corporate Sustainability Assessment Period Review dates: _____ to _____

1.0 Organizational Policies and Procedures

1.1 Does your organization have a published corporate sustainability statement that addresses key economic, environmental, and social concerns, and defines the vision, mission, and values?

Yes ☐   No ☐

1.2 Does your organization have an organizational chart that highlights key positions that oversee the organization's corporate sustainability plan?

Yes ☐   No ☐

1.3 Does your organization have a published overview for this sustainability plan?

Yes ☐   No ☐

2.0 Project Improvement Teams for Corporate Sustainability Planning

2.1 Total employee population:

2.2 Project Teams

Name of Project Team	Employee Projects				Functional Area Team (Check Area)						
	Hours	Number of Participants	Date of Project Completion		Sales & Marketing Distribution	Human Resources	Production Engineering/ Maintenance	Finance/ Accounting	Adminis- tration	Shipping/ Receiving	Other

Forms can be downloaded from the CD-ROM located inside the back cover of this book.

3.0 Customers/Suppliers/Partners
3.1 List key customers   Number of key customers _____

Key Customer Names	Date Customer Relationship Began	Length of Time as a Customer	Unique Sustainability Requirements

3.2 List key suppliers/partners   Number of key suppliers/partners _____

Key Supplier/ Partner Names	Date Partnership Began	Length of Time as a Supplier/Partner	Unique Sustainability Requirements

4.0 Corporate Sustainability Activities

List other corporate sustainability activities that may have been carried out in your organization during this assessment review period.

Activity	Objective

5.0 Corporate Sustainability Training

5.1 Does your organization have a training budget for corporate sustainability initiatives?

Yes ☐   No ☐

5.2 What was your annual training expenditure(s) for corporate sustainability projects during this assessment review period?

5.3 Did your organization present corporate sustainability initiative(s) to employees during this assessment review period?

Yes ☐   No ☐

If yes, please specify the initiative(s).

Internal and External Courses and Workshops	Hours	Number of Participants	Date of Training	Functional Area Team (Check Area)						
				Sales & Marketing Distribution	Human Resources	Production Engineering/ Maintenance	Finance/ Accounting	Adminis- tration	Shipping/ Receiving	Other

6.0 Corporate Sustainability Assessments

6.1 Does your organization conduct corporate sustainability assessments?

Yes ☐   No ☐

If yes, please specify the areas and frequency of the assessment(s) being conducted during this review period.

Areas	Frequency
Internal Assessments	
External Assessments	
Others	

7.0 Trends/ Improvements for the Organization's Corporate Sustainability Plan

7.1 Are trends of key sustainability initiatives being tracked regularly?

Yes ☐   No ☐

If yes, list and collect documents.

Documents	How often tracked?

7.2 What are your organizational challenges regarding corporate sustainability?

Organizational Challenges
Competitive Environment
Strategic Challenges
Performance Challenges

NOTES

Seven Steps for Successful Assessment Implementation and Manual Use

The following seven steps will further explain how this manual will be useful in simplifying the assessment process for the organization.

Step One   Complete the Organizational Overview

The assessment team administrator and senior staff should complete the organizational overview (pages 14–18) before the team(s) conduct the corporate sustainability assessment. The organizational overview is the most appropriate starting point for the assessment and will provide a snapshot of the organization's sustainability initiatives before the team(s) begin the assessment process. The information collected in the organizational overview should be used to identify potential issues and challenges. In addition, it may be used for an initial self-assessment.

Step Two   Review Questions

Following the description of the category are corporate sustainability questions that have been simplified so they are more understandable and user-friendly. This allows a clearer and more precise corporate sustainability assessment to be conducted.

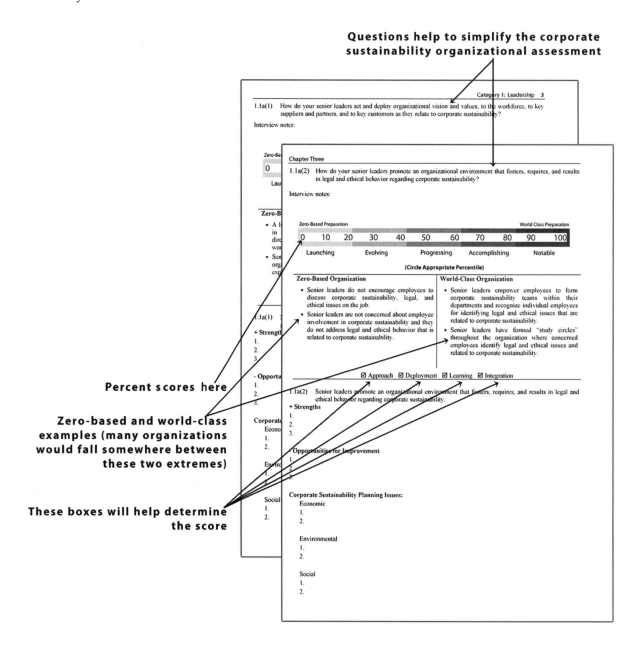

The questions should be posed to different levels of employees throughout the organization. The assessment team should divide this task among its members.

Step Three   Review Zero-Based and World-Class Examples

Before recording answers to the questions, review the examples of zero-based and world-class organizations' corporate sustainability initiatives that appear in the center of the page.

Below the examples appear four boxes labeled Approach, Deployment, Learning, and Integration. These boxes will aid in assessing the kinds of information and/or data the organization has in place and will aid the team in scoring the question (Refer to page 1).

Step Four   Make Interview Notes

Near the top of the page under each question is an interview notes section for recording answers to the questions given by employees as they are being interviewed by the assessment team. This data should be used to determine strengths, opportunities, and corporate sustainability strategic planning issues located in the lower portion of the page.

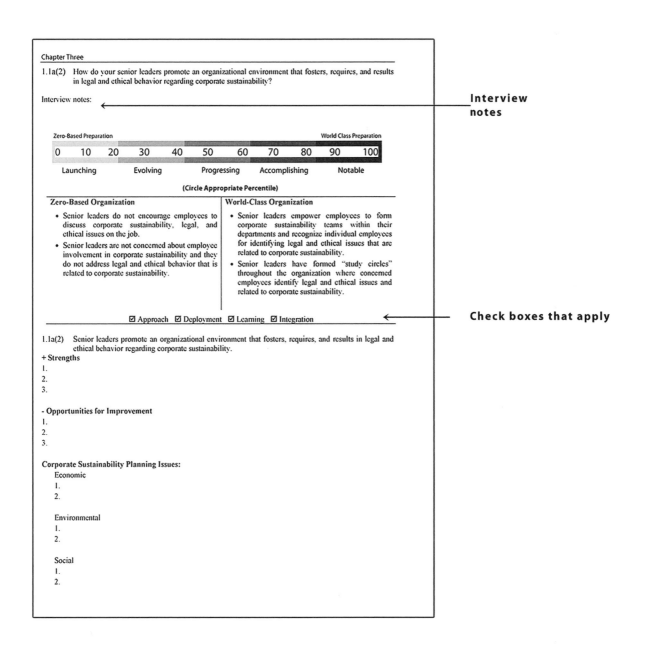

Step Five List Comments for Strengths and Improvement
On the lower half of the page, the question is restated. After the interviews are completed, review the interview notes. The team will then list strengths and opportunities for improvement. All comments should be written in short, complete sentences.

Step Six List Corporate Sustainability Strategic Planning Issues
After reviewing the interview notes, strengths, and opportunities for improvement, the assessment team should list any corporate sustainability planning issues. These planning issues are divided into three dimensions: Economic, Environmental, and Social.

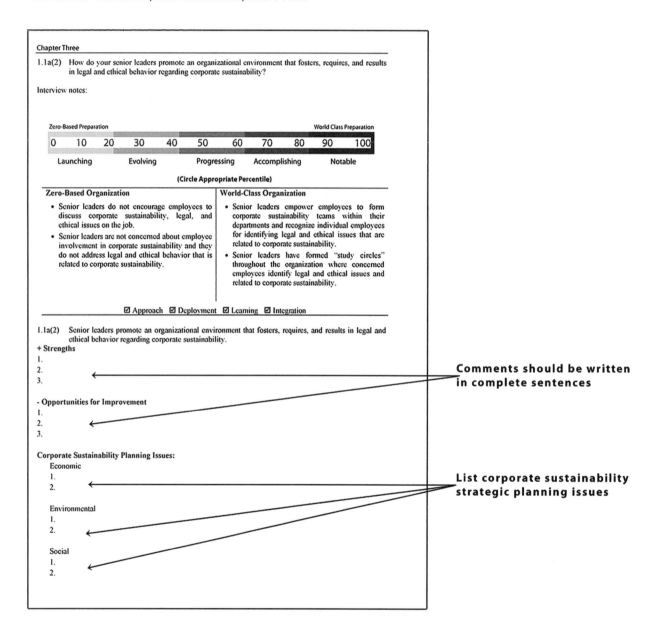

Chapter Three

1.1a(2) How do your senior leaders promote an organizational environment that fosters, requires, and results in legal and ethical behavior regarding corporate sustainability?

Interview notes:

Zero-Based Preparation · · · World Class Preparation

0 10 20 30 40 50 60 70 80 90 100

Launching · · · Evolving · · · Progressing · · · Accomplishing · · · Notable

(Circle Appropriate Percentile)

Zero-Based Organization	World-Class Organization
• Senior leaders do not encourage employees to discuss corporate sustainability, legal, and ethical issues on the job. • Senior leaders are not concerned about employee involvement in corporate sustainability and they do not address legal and ethical behavior that is related to corporate sustainability.	• Senior leaders empower employees to form corporate sustainability teams within their departments and recognize individual employees for identifying legal and ethical issues that are related to corporate sustainability. • Senior leaders have formed "study circles" throughout the organization where concerned employees identify legal and ethical issues and related to corporate sustainability.

☑ Approach ☑ Deployment ☑ Learning ☑ Integration

1.1a(2) Senior leaders promote an organizational environment that fosters, requires, and results in legal and ethical behavior regarding corporate sustainability.

+ Strengths
1.
2.
3.

- Opportunities for Improvement
1.
2.
3.

Corporate Sustainability Planning Issues:
Economic
1.
2.

Environmental
1.
2.

Social
1.
2.

Comments should be written in complete sentences

List corporate sustainability strategic planning issues

Step Seven   Score Assessment Items
The assessment is broken down into seven sustainability categories:

1. Leadership
2. Strategic Planning
3. Customer Focus
4. Measurement, Analysis, and Knowledge Management
5. Workforce Focus
6. Process Management
7. Results

These seven categories are divided into 18 assessment items (that is, 1.1, 1.2, 2.1, 2.2) and the 18 assessment items are broken down into 89 areas (that is, 1.1a(1), 1.1b). The percent score is refl ective of the strengths and opportunities for improvement of the areas within each assessment item. Thus, throughout the assessment, all 18 items will obtain a percent score. All assessment item percent scores will be transferred to the *Corporate Sustainability Score Sheet* located at the end of Chapter 9. A graph illustrating the *hierarchy* of

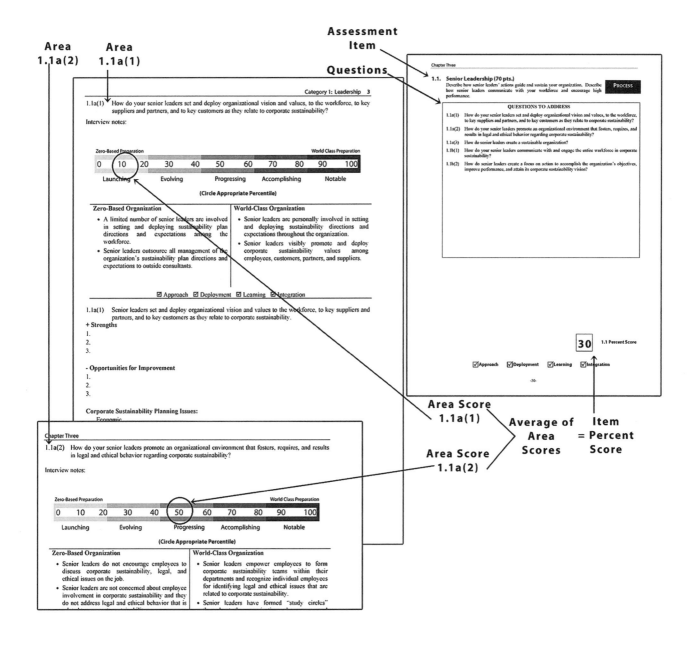

corporate sustainability assessment needs visually presents the percent scores of each assessment category. This graph follows the Corporate Sustainability Score sheet at the end of Chapter 9.

The assessment scores will ultimately be reviewed, prioritized, and transformed into actionable strategies for corporate sustainability improvement, and a corporate sustainability plan can be developed. The transformation process for consolidating corporate sustainability assessment fi ndings into a corporate sustainability plan is explained in detail in Chapter 10 of the manual. All assessment documents featured in this manual are available on the CD-ROM included inside the back cover.

3 Category 1
Leadership

1 Leadership (120 pts.)[11]

The *Leadership* Category examines how your organization's senior leaders' personal actions guide and sustain your organization. Also examined are your organization's governance system and how your organization fulfills its legal, ethical, and societal responsibilities and supports its key communities.

 Forms can be downloaded from the CD-ROM located inside the back cover of this book.

1.1. Senior Leadership (70 pts.)

Describe how senior leaders' actions guide and sustain your organization. Describe how senior leaders communicate with your workforce and encourage high performance.

PROCESS

QUESTIONS TO ADDRESS

1.1a(1) How do your senior leaders set and deploy organizational vision and values, to the workforce, to key suppliers and partners, and to key customers as they relate to corporate sustainability?

1.1a(2) How do your senior leaders promote an organizational environment that fosters, requires, and results in legal and ethical behavior regarding corporate sustainability?

1.1a(3) How do senior leaders create a sustainable organization?

1.1b(1) How do your senior leaders communicate with and engage the entire workforce in corporate sustainability?

1.1b(2) How do senior leaders create a focus on action to accomplish the organization's objectives, improve performance, and attain its corporate sustainability vision?

1.1 Percent Score

☐ Approach ☐ Deployment ☐ Learning ☐ Integration

1.1a(1) How do your senior leaders set and deploy organizational vision and values, to the workforce, to key suppliers and partners, and to key customers as they relate to corporate sustainability?

Interview notes:

0	10	20	30	40	50	60	70	80	90	100

Launching   Evolving   Progressing   Accomplishing   Notable

(Circle Appropriate Percentile)

Zero-Based Organization

- A limited number of senior leaders are involved in setting and deploying sustainability plan directions and expectations among the workforce.

- Senior leaders outsource all management of the organization's sustainability plan directions and expectations to outside consultants.

World-Class Organization

- Senior leaders are personally involved in setting and deploying sustainability directions and expectations throughout the organization.

- Senior leaders visibly promote and deploy corporate sustainability values among employees, customers, partners, and suppliers.

☐ Approach   ☐ Deployment   ☐ Learning   ☐ Integration

1.1a(1) Senior leaders set and deploy organizational vision and values to the workforce, to key suppliers and partners, and to key customers as they relate to corporate sustainability.

+ Strengths

1.

2.

3.

– Opportunities for Improvement

1.

2.

3.

Corporate Sustainability Planning Issues:

Economic

1.

2.

Environmental

1.

2.

Social

1.

2.

1.1a(2)   How do your senior leaders promote an organizational environment that fosters, requires, and results in legal and ethical behavior regarding corporate sustainability?

Interview notes:

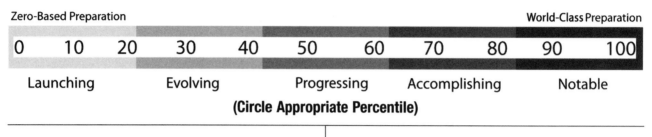

Zero-Based Preparation   **World-Class Preparation**

| 0 | 10 | 20 | 30 | 40 | 50 | 60 | 70 | 80 | 90 | 100 |

Launching   Evolving   Progressing   Accomplishing   Notable

(Circle Appropriate Percentile)

Zero-Based Organization

- Senior leaders do not encourage employees to discuss corporate sustainability, legal, and ethical issues on the job.
- Senior leaders are not concerned about employee involvement in corporate sustainability and they do not address legal and ethical behavior that is related to corporate sustainability.

World-Class Organization

- Senior leaders empower employees to form corporate sustainability teams within their departments and recognize individual employees for identifying legal and ethical issues that are related to corporate sustainability.
- Senior leaders have formed *study circles* throughout the organization where concerned employees identify legal and ethical issues related to corporate sustainability.

☐ **Approach**   ☐ **Deployment**   ☐ **Learning**   ☐ **Integration**

1.1a(2)   Senior leaders promote an organizational environment that fosters, requires, and results in legal and ethical behavior regarding corporate sustainability.

+ Strengths

1.
2.
3.

– Opportunities for Improvement

1.
2.
3.

Corporate Sustainability Planning Issues:

Economic

1.
2.

Environmental

1.
2.

Social

1.
2.

1.1a(3) How do senior leaders create a sustainable organization?

Interview notes:

Zero-Based Preparation   World-Class Preparation

| 0 | 10 | 20 | 30 | 40 | 50 | 60 | 70 | 80 | 90 | 100 |

Launching   Evolving   Progressing   Accomplishing   Notable

(Circle Appropriate Percentile)

Zero-Based Organization

- Senior leaders have no interest in ensuring that the organization is sustainable for employees, customers, and suppliers.
- Senior leaders do not associate the identification of sustainability issues and vulnerabilities as a longer-term initiative for stockholders and stakeholders.

World-Class Organization

- Senior leaders reward managers and supervisors who have sustainability plans documented and in place within their areas of responsibility.
- Organization conducts annual corporate sustainability self-assessments and senior leadership uses results to gauge ongoing progress in sustainability efforts throughout the organization.

☐ Approach   ☐ Deployment   ☐ Learning   ☐ Integration

1.1a(3)   Senior leaders create a sustainable organization.

+ Strengths

1.

2.

3.

– Opportunities for Improvement

1.

2.

3.

Corporate Sustainability Planning Issues:

Economic

1.

2.

Environmental

1.

2.

Social

1.

2.

1.1b(1)   How do your senior leaders communicate with and engage the entire workforce in corporate sustainability?

Interview notes:

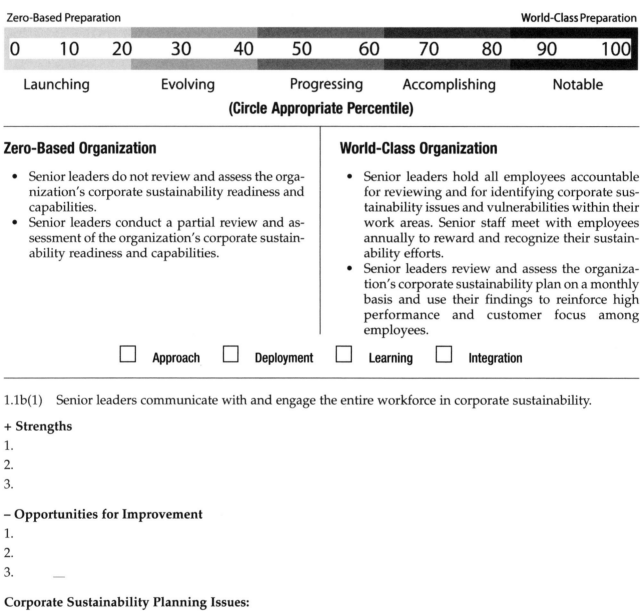

Zero-Based Preparation | World-Class Preparation

| 0 | 10 | 20 | 30 | 40 | 50 | 60 | 70 | 80 | 90 | 100 |

Launching   Evolving   Progressing   Accomplishing   Notable

(Circle Appropriate Percentile)

Zero-Based Organization

- Senior leaders do not review and assess the organization's corporate sustainability readiness and capabilities.
- Senior leaders conduct a partial review and assessment of the organization's corporate sustainability readiness and capabilities.

World-Class Organization

- Senior leaders hold all employees accountable for reviewing and for identifying corporate sustainability issues and vulnerabilities within their work areas. Senior staff meet with employees annually to reward and recognize their sustainability efforts.
- Senior leaders review and assess the organization's corporate sustainability plan on a monthly basis and use their findings to reinforce high performance and customer focus among employees.

☐ Approach   ☐ Deployment   ☐ Learning   ☐ Integration

1.1b(1)   Senior leaders communicate with and engage the entire workforce in corporate sustainability.

+ Strengths

1.

2.

3.

– Opportunities for Improvement

1.

2.

3.   __

Corporate Sustainability Planning Issues:

Economic

1.

2.

Environmental

1.

2.

Social

1.

2.

1.1b(2)   How do senior leaders create a focus on action to accomplish the organization's objectives, improve performance, and attain its corporate sustainability vision?

Interview notes:

Zero-Based Preparation   World-Class Preparation

| 0 | 10 | 20 | 30 | 40 | 50 | 60 | 70 | 80 | 90 | 100 |

Launching   Evolving   Progressing   Accomplishing   Notable

(Circle Appropriate Percentile)

Zero-Based Organization

- Senior leaders have not identified key corporate sustainability performance measures to review throughout the organization.
- Senior leaders have identified five key corporate sustainability performance measures but conduct random reviews on an inconsistent basis.

World-Class Organization

- Senior leaders review on a monthly basis their technological and organizational innovations that relate to a sustainable environment for the workforce and other key stakeholders.
- Senior leaders incorporate the use of Six Sigma and Lean technology to improve performance, eliminate waste, and reduce cycle-time within key sustainability efforts corporate-wide.

☐ Approach   ☐ Deployment   ☐ Learning   ☐ Integration

1.1b(2)   Senior leaders create a focus on action to accomplish the organization's objectives, improve performance, and attain its corporate sustainability vision.

+ Strengths

1.

2.

3.

– Opportunities for Improvement

1.

2.

3.

Corporate Sustainability Planning Issues:

Economic

   1.

   2.

Environmental

   1.

   2.

Social

   1.

   2.

1.2 Governance and Societal Responsibilities (50 pts.)

Describe your organization's governance system and approach to leadership improvement. Describe how your organization assures legal and ethical behavior, fulfills its societal responsibilities, and supports its key communities.

PROCESS

QUESTIONS TO ADDRESS

1.2a(1)   How does your organization review and achieve accountability for management's actions, fiscal accountability, transparency in operations, independence in internal/external audits, and protecting stakeholder/stockholder interests?

1.2a(2)   How does your organization evaluate the performance of senior leaders and the governance board?

1.2b(1)   How does your organization address any adverse impacts on society of your products and operations?

1.2b(2)   How does your organization promote and ensure ethical behavior in your transactions?

1.2c(1)   How does your organization consider sustainability planning as part of your strategy and daily operations?

1.2c(2)   How does your organization actively support and strengthen sustainability efforts in communities in which business is conducted?

1.2 Percent Score

☐ Approach   ☐ Deployment   ☐ Learning   ☐ Integration

1.2a(1) How does your organization review and achieve accountability for management's actions, fiscal accountability, transparency in operations, independence in internal/external audits, and protecting stakeholder/ stockholder interests?

Interview notes:

World-Class Preparation

| 0 | 10 | 20 | 30 | 40 | 50 | 60 | 70 | 80 | 90 | 100 |

Launching   Evolving   Progressing   Accomplishing   Notable

(Circle Appropriate Percentile)

Zero-Based Organization

- Organization does not address corporate sustainability governance issues on its products, services, and operations and does not consider these issues to be important.
- Organization does not address or detail corporate sustainability governance issues on its products, services, and operations.

World-Class Organization

- Organization developed a brochure describing key governance issues such as fiscal accountability, audits, and transparency issues related to operations, and distributes the brochure to key suppliers, partners, customers, and stakeholders.
- Organization holds public forums with communities where business is conducted to address corporate sustainability governance concerns on products, services, and operations.

☐ Approach   ☐ Deployment   ☐ Learning   ☐ Integration

1.2a(1) The organization reviews and achieves accountability for management's actions, fiscal accountability, transparency in operations, independence in internal/external audits, and protection of stakeholder/ stockholder interests.

+ Strengths
1.
2.
3.

– Opportunities for Improvement
1.
2.
3.

Corporate Sustainability Planning Issues:
Economic
1.
2.
Environmental
1.
2.
Social
1.
2.

1.2a(2)   How does your organization evaluate the performance of senior leaders and the governance board?

Interview notes:

Zero-Based Preparation   World-Class Preparation

| 0 | 10 | 20 | 30 | 40 | 50 | 60 | 70 | 80 | 90 | 100 |

Launching   Evolving   Progressing   Accomplishing   Notable

(Circle Appropriate Percentile)

Zero-Based Organization

- Organization does not evaluate the performance of senior leaders and the governance board as they relate to corporate sustainability.
- Organization does not address and is not concerned with senior leadership and board effectiveness regarding sustainability issues.

World-Class Organization

- Organization surveys the workforce and key stakeholders to gauge senior leadership and board effectiveness regarding corporate sustainability issues.
- Organization uses its website and 24-hour response line telephone system to allow the public to log in and register corporate sustainability concerns with current and future products, services, and operations and senior leadership and board effectiveness in leading their corporate sustainability efforts.

☐ Approach   ☐ Deployment   ☐ Learning   ☐ Integration

1.2a(2)   The organization evaluates the performance of senior leaders and the governance board.

+ Strengths

1.

2.

3.

– Opportunities for Improvement

1.

2.

3.

Corporate Sustainability Planning Issues:

Economic

1.

2.

Environmental

1.

2.

Social

1.

2.

1.2b(1)   How does your organization address any adverse impacts on society of your products and operations?
Interview notes:

Zero-Based Preparation   World-Class Preparation

| 0 | 10 | 20 | 30 | 40 | 50 | 60 | 70 | 80 | 90 | 100 |

Launching   Evolving   Progressing   Accomplishing   Notable

(Circle Appropriate Percentile)

Zero-Based Organization

- Organization does not have a plan in place to address any adverse impacts on society from their products and operations.
- Organization has no processes in place to ensure that natural resources are being conserved, regulatory and legal requirements are being met and/or exceeded, and that effective supply chain management processes are in place and are meeting key societal and environmental concerns.

World-Class Organization

- Organization has developed a code of ethical conduct regarding corporate sustainability issues that impact products, services, and operations. This statement is distributed to all employees, suppliers, partners, customers, and key stakeholders.
- Organization identifies and addresses all key and critical corporate sustainability issues that affect stakeholder transactions and interactions.

☐ Approach   ☐ Deployment   ☐ Learning   ☐ Integration

1.2b(1)   The organization addresses any adverse impacts on society of its products and operations.

+ Strengths
1.
2.
3.

– Opportunities for Improvement
1.
2.
3.

Corporate Sustainability Planning Issues:
Economic
1.
2.
Environmental
1.
2.
Social
1.
2.

1.2b(2)   How does your organization promote and ensure ethical behavior in your transactions?

Interview notes:

| 0 | 10 | 20 | 30 | 40 | 50 | 60 | 70 | 80 | 90 | 100 |

| Launching | Evolving | Progressing | Accomplishing | Notable |

(Circle Appropriate Percentile)

Zero-Based Organization

- Organization does not have policies and procedures in place to assure that ethical behavior in all transactions is being followed.
- Organization has not formally addressed ethics issues that relate to product, service, and operational transactions.

World-Class Organization

- Organization formally recognizes and rewards employees who display ethical conduct in various products, service, and operational transactions.
- Organization promotes transparency in all product/service transactions and promotes employees who exhibit notable ethical behavior in conducting key operational transactions.

☐ Approach   ☐ Deployment   ☐ Learning   ☐ Integration

1.2b(2)   The organization promotes and assures ethical behavior in transactions.

+ Strengths

1.

2.

3.

– Opportunities for Improvement

1.

2.

3.

Corporate Sustainability Planning Issues:

Economic

1.

2.

Environmental

1.

2.

Social

1.

2.

1.2c(1)   How does your organization consider sustainability planning as part of your strategy and daily operations?

Interview notes:

Zero-Based Preparation   World-Class Preparation

0	10	20	30	40	50	60	70	80	90	100

Launching   Evolving   Progressing   Accomplishing   Notable

(Circle Appropriate Percentile)

Zero-Based Organization

- Organization does not consider sustainability planning issues as part of their corporate strategy and daily operations.
- Organization does not support sustainability efforts among employees, suppliers, customers, stakeholders, and community groups.

World-Class Organization

- Organization has identified key short- and longer-term sustainability goals in their corporate strategic plan and rewards employees who meet and/or exceed their corporate sustainability goals within their daily operations.
- Organization formally promotes corporate sustainability in its strategic plan and daily operations.

☐ Approach   ☐ Deployment   ☐ Learning   ☐ Integration

1.2c(1)   The organization considers sustainability planning as part of the strategy and daily operations.

+ Strengths

1.

2.

3.

– Opportunities for Improvement

1.

2.

3.

Corporate Sustainability Planning Issues:

Economic

1.

2.

Environmental

1.

2.

Social

1.

2.

1.2c(2) How does your organization actively support and strengthen sustainability efforts in communities in which business is conducted?

Interview notes:

Zero-Based Preparation   World-Class Preparation

| 0 | 10 | 20 | 30 | 40 | 50 | 60 | 70 | 80 | 90 | 100 |

Launching   Evolving   Progressing   Accomplishing   Notable

(Circle Appropriate Percentile)

Zero-Based Organization

- Organization does not contribute money or employee volunteers for sustainability initiatives within the communities in which business is conducted.
- Organization offers no community involvement regarding sustainability efforts.

World-Class Organization

- Organization recognizes employees who promote sustainability issues in local, state, national, and industry organizations.
- Organization provides extra pay incentives for employees who volunteer their time to promote sustainability efforts within communities where business is conducted.

☐ Approach   ☐ Deployment   ☐ Learning   ☐ Integration

1.2c(2) The organization actively supports and strengthens sustainability efforts in communities in which business is conducted.

+ Strengths

1.

2.

3.

– Opportunities for Improvement

1.

2.

3.

Corporate Sustainability Planning Issues:

Economic

1.

2.

Environmental

1.

2.

Social

1.

2.

NOTES

4 Category 2: Strategic Planning

2 Strategic Planning (85 pts.)[12]

The *Strategic Planning* Category examines how your organization develops strategic objectives and action plans for corporate sustainability. Also examined are how your chosen strategic objectives and action plans are deployed and changed if circumstances require, and how progress is measured.

Forms can be downloaded from the CD-ROM located inside the back cover of this book.

2.1 Strategy Development (40 pts.)

Describe how your organization establishes its corporate sustainability strategy to address its strategic challenges and leverage its strategic advantages. Summarize your organization's key strategic objectives and their related goals.

PROCESS

QUESTIONS TO ADDRESS

2.1a(1) How does your organization conduct strategic planning for corporate sustainability?

2.1a(2) How does your organization ensure that strategic planning addresses key corporate sustainability factors (that is customer/market needs, competitive environment, technology needs, human resources, redirecting resources, environmental issues, financial risks, societal risks, national/global economy changes, partner/supply chain needs, and human rights)?

2.1b(1) What are your organization's key strategic objectives for corporate sustainability and your timetable for accomplishing them?

2.1b(2) How does your organization address your strategic challenges and advantages?

2.1 Percent Score

☐ Approach   ☐ Deployment   ☐ Learning   ☐ Integration

2.1a(1) How does your organization conduct strategic planning for corporate sustainability?

Interview notes:

Zero-Based Preparation   World-Class Preparation

| 0 | 10 | 20 | 30 | 40 | 50 | 60 | 70 | 80 | 90 | 100 |

| Launching | Evolving | Progressing | Accomplishing | Notable |

(Circle Appropriate Percentile)

Zero-Based Organization

- Organization does not have an overall strategic planning process in place for corporate sustainability.
- Organization has not developed a vision and identified strategic objectives to implement a plan for corporate sustainability.

World-Class Organization

- Organization has each division identify and develop short- and longer-term objectives for corporate sustainability. All division plans are merged into an organization-wide plan for sustainability.
- Organization involves input from all employee levels when developing an overall strategic planning process for corporate sustainability.

☐ Approach   ☐ Deployment   ☐ Learning   ☐ Integration

2.1a(1) The organization conducts strategic planning for corporate sustainability.

+ Strengths

1.

2.

3.

– Opportunities for Improvement

1.

2.

3.

Corporate Sustainability Planning Issues:

Economic

1.

2.

Environmental

1.

2.

Social

1.

2.

2.1a(2)   How does your organization ensure that strategic planning addresses key corporate sustainability factors (that is, customer/market needs, competitive environment, technology needs, human resources, redirecting resources, environmental issues, financial risks, societal risks, national/global economy changes, partner/supply chain needs, and human rights)?

Interview notes:

Zero-Based Preparation   World-Class Preparation

| 0 | 10 | 20 | 30 | 40 | 50 | 60 | 70 | 80 | 90 | 100 |

Launching   Evolving   Progressing   Accomplishing   Notable

(Circle Appropriate Percentile)

Zero-Based Organization

- Organization has not considered key corporate sustainability factors in its strategic plan such as corporate governance, risk and crisis man-age-ment, environmental performance (eco-efficiency), human capital development, and labor practices.
- Organization has not identified key corporate sustainability factors to develop a planning approach that will ensure sustainability within its operations in case of a major business disruption.

World-Class Organization

- Organization has a strategic plan to manage corporate sustainability issues and to mitigate future risks for the organization.
- Organization's strategic plan for corporate sustainability addresses increased technology needs, identification of product, service, and operational risks, and redirection of financial, environmental, and human resources.

☐ Approach   ☐ Deployment   ☐ Learning   ☐ Integration

2.1a(2)   The organization addresses key corporate sustainability factors in its strategic plan.

+ Strengths
1.
2.
3.

– Opportunities for Improvement
1.
2.
3.

Corporate Sustainability Planning Issues:
Economic
1.
2.
Environmental
1.
2.
Social
1.
2.

2.1b(1) What are your organization's key strategic objectives for corporate sustainability and your timetable for accomplishing them?

Interview notes:

| 0 | 10 | 20 | 30 | 40 | 50 | 60 | 70 | 80 | 90 | 100 |

Launching   Evolving   Progressing   Accomplishing   Notable

(Circle Appropriate Percentile)

Zero-Based Organization

- Organization has not identified key strategic objectives for corporate sustainability.
- Organization does not clearly define its strategic objectives and have a timetable in place to address corporate sustainability.

World-Class Organization

- Organization's key strategic objectives for corporate sustainability focus on human rights, corporate risks and regulations, environmental improvements, community investments, green planning, diversity, and economic value generation that addresses revenue and operating costs.
- Organization has prepared a timetable for accomplishing a corporate sustainability plan and shares it with all employee levels, key customers and suppliers, and key stakeholders.

☐ Approach ☐ Deployment ☐ Learning ☐ Integration

2.1b(1) The organization has key strategic objectives for corporate sustainability and a timetable for accomplishing them.

+ Strengths
1.
2.
3.

– Opportunities for Improvement
1.
2.
3.

Corporate Sustainability Planning Issues:
Economic
1.
2.
Environmental
1.
2.
Social
1.
2.

2.1b(2)   How does your organization address your strategic challenges and advantages?

Interview notes:

Zero-Based Preparation   World-Class Preparation

| 0 | 10 | 20 | 30 | 40 | 50 | 60 | 70 | 80 | 90 | 100 |

Launching   Evolving   Progressing   Accomplishing   Notable

(Circle Appropriate Percentile)

Zero-Based Organization

- Organization does not align strategic objectives for corporate sustainability with its short- and long-term business plans and goals and ensure that key stakeholders' sustainability needs are addressed.
- Organization does not focus on specific sustainability challenges and stakeholder needs when identifying and developing strategic objectives for corporate sustainability.

World-Class Organization

- Organization ensures that its strategic objectives for corporate sustainability balance the needs of all employees, key suppliers, partners, and customers.
- Organization addresses strategic corporate sustainability objectives that are most important to continuation of business success and overall business operations.

☐ Approach   ☐ Deployment   ☐ Learning   ☐ Integration

2.1b(2)   The organization's strategic challenges and advantages are addressed.

+ Strengths

1.

2.

3.

– Opportunities for Improvement

1.

2.

3.

Corporate Sustainability Planning Issues:

Economic

1.

2.

Environmental

1.

2.

Social

1.

2.

2.2 Strategy Deployment (45 pts.)

Describe how your organization converts its strategic objectives into action plans. Summarize your organization's action plans, how they are deployed, and key action plan performance measures or indicators. Project your organization's future performance relative to key comparisons on these performance measures or indicators.

PROCESS

QUESTIONS TO ADDRESS

2.2a(1) What are your organization's key short- and longer-term action plans?

2.2a(2) How does your organization develop and deploy action plans throughout the workforce and to key suppliers and partners?

2.2a(3) How does your organization ensure that financial and other resources are available to support the accomplishment of corporate sustainability action plans while meeting current obligations?

2.2a(4) How does your organization establish and deploy modified action plans for corporate sustainability?

2.2a(5) What are your organization's key human resource plans that derive from short- and longer-term corporate sustainability strategic objectives and action plans?

2.2a(6) What are your organization's key performance measures or indicators for tracking the achievement and effectiveness of corporate sustainability action plans?

2.2b What are your organization's key performance measures and projections for short- and longer-term planning time horizons for corporate sustainability?

2.2 Percent Score

☐ Approach ☐ Deployment ☐ Learning ☐ Integration

2.2a(1)   What are your organization's key short- and longer-term action plans?

Interview notes:

Zero-Based Preparation   World-Class Preparation

| 0 | 10 | 20 | 30 | 40 | 50 | 60 | 70 | 80 | 90 | 100 |

Launching   Evolving   Progressing   Accomplishing   Notable

(Circle Appropriate Percentile)

Zero-Based Organization

- Organization does not provide either financial or human resources to develop and deploy action plans to achieve corporate sustainability goals and objectives.
- Organization has developed corporate sustainability action plans but does not gauge progress toward meeting these goals.

World-Class Organization

- Organization's senior leadership sets and communicates corporate sustainability goals, directions, and action plans to all employee levels.
- Organization provides financial and human resources to develop and deploy action plans to achieve key corporate sustainability strategic objectives.

☐ Approach   ☐ Deployment   ☐ Learning   ☐ Integration

2.2a(1)   The organization develops and deploys key short- and longer-term action plans.

+ Strengths

1.

2.

3.

– Opportunities for Improvement

1.

2.

3.

Corporate Sustainability Planning Issues:

Economic

1.

2.

Environmental

1.

2.

Social

1.

2.

2.2a(2)   How does your organization develop and deploy action plans throughout the workforce and to key suppliers and partners?

Interview notes:

Zero-Based Preparation   World-Class Preparation

| 0 | 10 | 20 | 30 | 40 | 50 | 60 | 70 | 80 | 90 | 100 |

Launching   Evolving   Progressing   Accomplishing   Notable

(Circle Appropriate Percentile)

Zero-Based Organization

- Organization has no action plans developed for corporate sustainability.
- Organization collects anecdotal information regarding sustainability efforts. Limited action plans are developed for corporate sustainability and do not involve the workforce, key suppliers, and partners.

World-Class Organization

- Organization's key short- and longer-term action plans for corporate sustainability include economic, environmental, and social initiatives, and involve all workforce levels and key suppliers and partners.
- Organization has conducted a corporate sustainability assessment that involved the workforce, key suppliers, customers, and partners and developed short- and long-term action plans that address key sustainability issues.

☐ Approach   ☐ Deployment   ☐ Learning   ☐ Integration

2.2a(2)   The organization develops and deploys action plans throughout the workforce and to key suppliers and partners.

+ Strengths
1.
2.
3.

– Opportunities for Improvement
1.
2.
3.

Corporate Sustainability Planning Issues:
Economic
1.
2.
Environmental
1.
2.
Social
1.
2.

2.2a(3)   How does your organization ensure that financial and other resources are available to support the accomplishment of corporate sustainability action plans while meeting current obligations?

Interview notes:

Zero-Based Preparation   World-Class Preparation

| 0 | 10 | 20 | 30 | 40 | 50 | 60 | 70 | 80 | 90 | 100 |

Launching   Evolving   Progressing   Accomplishing   Notable

(Circle Appropriate Percentile)

Zero-Based Organization

- Organization does not identify financial and/or other resources to support its corporate sustainability efforts and has no formal action plans in place.
- Organization is not concerned with budgeting for corporate sustainability and seldom identifies other resources to address sustainability opportunities for the organization.

World-Class Organization

- Organization has a formal corporate sustainability plan with identified financial and other resources committed to ensure accomplishment of action plans.
- Organization requires all divisions to formally include budget dollars and other resources in their sustainability plans.

☐ Approach   ☐ Deployment   ☐ Learning   ☐ Integration

2.2a(3)   The organization ensures that financial and other resources are available to support corporate sustainability action plans while meeting current obligations.

+ Strengths

1.

2.

3.

– Opportunities for Improvement

1.

2.

3.

Corporate Sustainability Planning Issues:

Economic

1.

2.

Environmental

1.

2.

Social

1.

2.

2.2a(4)   How does your organization establish and deploy modified action plans for corporate sustainability?

Interview notes:

Zero-Based Preparation   World-Class Preparation

| 0 | 10 | 20 | 30 | 40 | 50 | 60 | 70 | 80 | 90 | 100 |

Launching   Evolving   Progressing   Accomplishing   Notable

(Circle Appropriate Percentile)

Zero-Based Organization

- Organization has no formal process in place to establish and deploy modified action plans for corporate sustainability.
- Organization does not modify action plans for corporate sustainability. All plan changes are addressed in future planning sessions.

World-Class Organization

- Organization has a format online to establish and deploy modified action plans for corporate sustainability throughout the organization.
- All corporate sustainability action plans are reviewed by selected employees, key suppliers, and customers before any modifications are made and distributed.

☐ Approach   ☐ Deployment   ☐ Learning   ☐ Integration

2.2a(4)   The organization establishes and deploys modified action plans for corporate sustainability.

+ Strengths

1.

2.

3.

– Opportunities for Improvement

1.

2.

3.

Corporate Sustainability Planning Issues:

Economic

1.

2.

Environmental

1.

2.

Social

1.

2.

2.2a(5)   What are your organization's key human resource plans that derive from short- and longer-term corporate sustainability strategic objectives and action plans?

Interview notes:

Zero-Based Preparation   World-Class Preparation

| 0 | 10 | 20 | 30 | 40 | 50 | 60 | 70 | 80 | 90 | 100 |

Launching   Evolving   Progressing   Accomplishing   Notable

(Circle Appropriate Percentile)

Zero-Based Organization

- Organization does not have a human resource plan that addresses corporate sustainability.
- Organization has not aligned its corporate sustainability goals and objectives with its human resource plan.

World-Class Organization

- Organization has developed a human resource plan for corporate sustainability that is aligned with short- and long-term strategic plans and goals.
- Organization involves cross-functional employee teams to develop a corporate sustainability human resource plan. The plan is aligned with the organization's strategic goals and objectives.

☐ Approach   ☐ Deployment   ☐ Learning   ☐ Integration

2.2a(5)   The organization's key human resource plans derive from short- and longer-term corporate sustainability strategic objectives and action plans.

+ Strengths
1.
2.
3.

– Opportunities for Improvement
1.
2.
3.

Corporate Sustainability Planning Issues:
Economic
1.
2.
Environmental
1.
2.
Social
1.
2.

2.2a(6)   What are your organization's key performance measures or indicators for tracking the achievement and effectiveness of corporate sustainability action plans?

Interview notes:

Zero-Based Preparation   World-Class Preparation

| 0 | 10 | 20 | 30 | 40 | 50 | 60 | 70 | 80 | 90 | 100 |

Launching   Evolving   Progressing   Accomplishing   Notable

(Circle Appropriate Percentile)

Zero-Based Organization

- Organization does not track progress on its corporate sustainability action plans.
- Organization has no performance measures in place to gauge corporate sustainability action plan progress.

World-Class Organization

- Organization has identified a set of performance measures to track its corporate sustainability action plans.
- Organization has conducted a corporate sustainability assessment and identified three indicators to track progress regarding action plans. These include cycle time, completion date of action plans, and impact on the organization.

☐ Approach   ☐ Deployment   ☐ Learning   ☐ Integration

2.2a(6)   The organization has key performance measures or indicators for tracking the achievement and effectiveness of corporate sustainability action plans.

+ Strengths

1.

2.

3.

- Opportunities for Improvement

1.

2.

3.

Corporate Sustainability Planning Issues:

Economic

1.

2.

Environmental

1.

2.

Social

1.

2.

2.2b   What are your organization's key performance measures and projections for short- and longer-term planning time horizons for corporate sustainability?

Interview notes:

Zero-Based Preparation   World-Class Preparation

| 0 | 10 | 20 | 30 | 40 | 50 | 60 | 70 | 80 | 90 | 100 |

Launching   Evolving   Progressing   Accomplishing   Notable

(Circle Appropriate Percentile)

Zero-Based Organization

- Organization does not use performance projections to gauge corporate sustainability progress.
- Organization uses no performance projections or indicators and does not compare its corporate sustainability performance against key benchmark goals and past performance.

World-Class Organization

- Organization's performance projections are used to improve its rate of improvement for corporate sustainability issues and serve as a key diagnostic management tool.
- Organization uses performance projections to gauge new and innovative corporate sustainability initiatives.

☐ Approach   ☐ Deployment   ☐ Learning   ☐ Integration

2.2b   The organization has key performance measures and projections for short- and longer-term planning time horizons for corporate sustainability.

+ Strengths

1.

2.

3.

– Opportunities for Improvement

1.

2.

3.

Corporate Sustainability Planning Issues:

Economic

1.

2.

Environmental

1.

2.

Social

1.

2.

NOTES

5 Category 3: Customer Focus

3 Customer Focus (85 pts.)[13]

The *Customer Focus* Category examines how your organization engages its customers for long-term marketplace success and corporate sustainability. This engagement strategy includes how your organization builds a customer-focused culture. Also examined is how your organization listens to the voice of its customers and uses this information to improve and identify opportunities for innovation for overall corporate sustainability.

 Forms can be downloaded from the CD-ROM located inside the back cover of this book.

3.1 Customer Engagement (40 pts.)

Describe how your organization determines product offerings and mechanisms to support customers' use of your products. Describe also how your organization builds a customer-focused culture.

PROCESS

QUESTIONS TO ADDRESS

3.1a(1) How does your organization identify and innovate product/service offerings to meet the requirements and exceed the expectations of your customer groups and market segments based on their sustainability needs?

3.1a(2) How does your organization determine key mechanisms to support use of sustainable products/services and enable customers to seek information and conduct business with you?

3.1a(3) How does your organization keep your approaches for identifying and innovating product/service sustainability offerings and for providing customer support current with business needs and directions?

3.1b(1) How does your organization create a culture that ensures a consistently positive and sustainable customer experience and contributes to customer engagement?

3.1b(2) How does your organization build and manage relationships with customers regarding sustainability issues?

3.1b(3) How does your organization keep approaches for creating a customer-focused culture and building customer relationships current with sustainability needs and directions?

3.1 Percent Score

☐ Approach ☐ Deployment ☐ Learning ☐ Integration

3.1a(1)   How does your organization identify and innovate product/service offerings to meet the requirements and exceed the expectations of your customer groups and market segments based on their sustainability needs?

Interview notes:

Zero-Based Preparation   World-Class Preparation

| 0 | 10 | 20 | 30 | 40 | 50 | 60 | 70 | 80 | 90 | 100 |

| Launching | Evolving | Progressing | Accomplishing | Notable |

(Circle Appropriate Percentile)

Zero-Based Organization

- Organization does not segment or survey customers and customer groups regarding their sustainability needs and expectations.
- Organization has no concern for segmenting customers regarding sustainability initiatives. All customers are treated the same regarding their corporate sustainability needs.

World-Class Organization

- Organization segments customer groups and market segments to determine and target application of their sustainability needs.
- Organization surveys customers and customer groups, aggregates the data, and determines the level of their sustainability needs based on results.

☐ Approach   ☐ Deployment   ☐ Learning   ☐ Integration

3.1a(1)   The organization identifies and innovates product/service offerings to meet the requirements and exceed the expectations of customer groups and market segments based on their sustainability needs.

+ Strengths
1.
2.
3.

– Opportunities for Improvement
1.
2.
3.

Corporate Sustainability Planning Issues:
Economic
1.
2.
Environmental
1.
2.
Social
1.
2.

3.1a(2)   How does your organization determine key mechanisms to support use of sustainable products/services and enable customers to seek information and conduct business with you?

Interview notes:

Zero-Based Preparation   World-Class Preparation

| 0 | 10 | 20 | 30 | 40 | 50 | 60 | 70 | 80 | 90 | 100 |

Launching   Evolving   Progressing   Accomplishing   Notable

(Circle Appropriate Percentile)

Zero-Based Organization

- Organization does not address corporate sustainability requirements and expectations with its customers.
- Organization has identified a limited number of key customers to interview concerning their requirements and expectations regarding corporate sustainability issues. The results of these interviews determine what sustainability issues will be deployed to all customers.

World-Class Organization

- Organization's customer-contact employees meet monthly with key customers to determine their requirements and expectations regarding sustainability issues.
- Organization conducts annual surveys and holds quarterly focus groups with key customers to determine their sustainability requirements and expectations.

☐ Approach   ☐ Deployment   ☐ Learning   ☐ Integration

3.1a(2)   The organization determines key mechanisms to support use of sustainable products/services and enable customers to seek information and conduct business.

+ Strengths
1.
2.
3.

– Opportunities for Improvement
1.
2.
3.

Corporate Sustainability Planning Issues:
Economic
1.
2.
Environmental
1.
2.
Social
1.
2.

3.1a(3)   How does your organization keep your approaches for identifying and innovating product/service sustainability offerings and for providing customer support current with business needs and directions?

Interview notes:

Zero-Based Preparation   World-Class Preparation

| 0 | 10 | 20 | 30 | 40 | 50 | 60 | 70 | 80 | 90 | 100 |

Launching   Evolving   Progressing   Accomplishing   Notable

(Circle Appropriate Percentile)

Zero-Based Organization

- Organization is not concerned with using listening posts to better understand customer concerns and expectations regarding sustainability issues. The organization has no concern for changing and incorporating current methods.
- Organization seldom changes its methods for gauging sustainability needs and directions for customers.

World-Class Organization

- Organization annually surveys international, federal, state, and local customers and markets to ensure that listening and learning methods for its customers are current with global standards for corporate sustainability offerings.
- Organization hosts annual focus groups of corporate sustainability subject-matter experts to ensure that its listening and learning methods are current and state of the art and that its product/service offerings are innovative and promote best sustainable practices.

☐ Approach   ☐ Deployment   ☐ Learning   ☐ Integration

3.1a(3)   The organization keeps approaches for identifying and innovating product/service sustainability offerings and for providing customer support current with business needs and directions.

+ Strengths
1.
2.
3.

– Opportunities for Improvement
1.
2.
3.

Corporate Sustainability Planning Issues:
Economic
1.
2.
Environmental
1.
2.
Social
1.
2.

3.1b(1)   How does your organization create a culture that ensures a consistently positive and sustainable customer experience and contributes to customer engagement?

Interview notes:

Zero-Based Preparation   World-Class Preparation

| 0 | 10 | 20 | 30 | 40 | 50 | 60 | 70 | 80 | 90 | 100 |

Launching   Evolving   Progressing   Accomplishing   Notable

(Circle Appropriate Percentile)

Zero-Based Organization

- Organization has no formal, nor consistent process in place to ensure a positive and sustainable customer experience.
- Organization is not concerned with customer retention and loyalty and makes limited efforts to create a sustainable customer base.

World-Class Organization

- Organization ensures customer retention and loyalty through its corporate sustainability efforts that are aligned with its product/service offerings.
- Organization promotes sustainability efforts and products among its customers to increase business and product brand loyalty within the industry sector.

☐ Approach   ☐ Deployment   ☐ Learning   ☐ Integration

3.1b(1)   The organization creates a culture that ensures a consistent, positive, and sustainable customer experience and contributes to customer engagement.

+ Strengths

1.

2.

3.

– Opportunities for Improvement

1.

2.

3.

Corporate Sustainability Planning Issues:

Economic

1.

2.

Environmental

1.

2.

Social

1.

2.

3.1b(2) How does your organization build and manage relationships with customers regarding sustainability issues?

Interview notes:

Zero-Based Preparation   World-Class Preparation

| 0 | 10 | 20 | 30 | 40 | 50 | 60 | 70 | 80 | 90 | 100 |

Launching   Evolving   Progressing   Accomplishing   Notable
(Circle Appropriate Percentile)

Zero-Based Organization	**World-Class Organization**
• Organization's senior staff are the only ones involved with customers to build relationships regarding sustainability issues. • Organization does not systematically identify and determine customer needs and expectations regarding sustainability issues and use findings to maintain and build ongoing relationships.	• Organization holds semi-annual roundtable discussions with key customers to build better customer relationships regarding corporate sustainability issues. • Organization conducts an annual customer forum for key customers to share and communicate the organization's sustainability plans and initiatives.

☐ Approach   ☐ Deployment   ☐ Learning   ☐ Integration

3.1b(2) The organization builds and manages relationships with customers regarding sustainability issues.

+ Strengths
1.
2.
3.

– Opportunities for Improvement
1.
2.
3.

Corporate Sustainability Planning Issues:

Economic
1.
2.

Environmental
1.
2.

Social
1.
2.

3.1b(3)   How does your organization keep approaches for creating a customer-focused culture and building customer relationships current with sustainability needs and directions?

Interview notes:

Zero-Based Preparation   World-Class Preparation

| 0 | 10 | 20 | 30 | 40 | 50 | 60 | 70 | 80 | 90 | 100 |

Launching   Evolving   Progressing   Accomplishing   Notable

(Circle Appropriate Percentile)

Zero-Based Organization

- Organization is not concerned with its approach to building relationships and providing customers access to current sustainability needs and directions.
- Organization does not address relationship management with customers regarding sustainability issues and directions.

World-Class Organization

- Organization conducts formal benchmarks to organizations known to have *best practice* corporate sustainability practices and approaches for customers. The organization uses its findings to validate its approaches.
- Organization uses industry focus groups to review and validate its approaches to building relationships and providing customers access to corporate sustainability issues and directions.

☐ **Approach**   ☐ **Deployment**   ☐ **Learning**   ☐ **Integration**

3.1b(3)   The organization's approaches for creating a customer-focused culture and building customer relationships are current with sustainability needs and directions.

+ Strengths
1.
2.
3.

– Opportunities for Improvement
1.
2.
3.

Corporate Sustainability Planning Issues:
Economic
1.
2.
Environmental
1.
2.
Social
1.
2.

3.2   Voice of the Customer (45 pts.)

Describe how your organization listens to your customers and acquires satisfaction and dissatisfaction information. Describe also how customer information is used to improve your marketplace success.

PROCESS

QUESTIONS TO ADDRESS

3.2a(1)   How does your organization obtain actionable information and feedback on your products/services and customer support and corporate sustainability efforts?

3.2a(2)   How does your organization listen to former customers, potential customers, and customers of competitors to obtain actionable information and to obtain feedback on products, customer support, transactions, and sustainability efforts?

3.2a(3)   How does your organization manage sustainability complaints?

3.2b(1)   How does your organization determine customer satisfaction and engagement regarding corporate sustainability efforts?

3.2b(2)   How does your organization obtain and use customer satisfaction with corporate sustainability efforts relative to their satisfaction with competitors?

3.2b(3)   How does your organization determine customer dissatisfaction with corporate sustainability efforts?

3.2c(1)   How does your organization use customer, market, and product offering information to identify current and anticipate future customer groups and market segments interested in sustainability efforts?

3.2c(2)   How does your organization use customer, market, and product/service offering information to identify and anticipate key customer sustainability requirements, changing sustainability expectations, and relative importance of sustainability for purchasing decisions?

3.2c(3)   How does your organization use customer, market, and product/service offering sustainability information to improve marketing, build a more customer-focused culture, and identify opportunities for innovation?

3.2c(4)   How does your organization keep approaches for customer listening, determination of customer satisfaction/dissatisfaction, and use of customer data current with sustainability needs and directions?

3.2 Percent Score

☐ Approach   ☐ Deployment   ☐ Learning   ☐ Integration

3.2a(1) How does your organization obtain actionable information and feedback on your products/services and customer support and corporate sustainability efforts?

Interview notes:

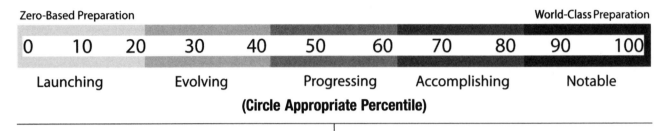

(Circle Appropriate Percentile)

Zero-Based Organization

- Organization performs limited follow-up with customers on product/service offerings and receives little feedback on the organization's corporate sustainability efforts.
- Organization does not engage customers through focus groups, surveys, complaint data, and information to use to validate ongoing satisfaction with corporate-wide sustainability efforts and to make actionable charges.

World-Class Organization

- Organization uses focus groups and customer appreciation councils to obtain information and feedback on products/services and customer support and corporate sustainability efforts.
- Organization uses several feedback modes to gauge customer satisfaction with sustainability efforts as they relate to product/service offerings which include focus groups with key customers, interviews with lost and potential customers, customer complaint data, and a win/loss analysis relative to competitors who offer similar sustainable products/services.

☐ Approach   ☐ Deployment   ☐ Learning   ☐ Integration

3.2a(1) The organization obtains actionable information and feedback on products/services and customer support and corporate sustainability efforts.

+ Strengths
1.
2.
3.

– Opportunities for Improvement
1.
2.
3.

Corporate Sustainability Planning Issues:
Economic
1.
2.
Environmental
1.
2.
Social
1.
2.

3.2a(2) How does your organization listen to former customers, potential customers, and customers of competitors to obtain actionable information and to obtain feedback on products, customer support, transactions, and sustainability efforts?

Interview notes:

Zero-Based Preparation   World-Class Preparation

| 0 | 10 | 20 | 30 | 40 | 50 | 60 | 70 | 80 | 90 | 100 |

Launching   Evolving   Progressing   Accomplishing   Notable

(Circle Appropriate Percentile)

Zero-Based Organization

- Organization has no formal process in place to seek and review feedback from former customers, potential customers, and customers of competitors.
- Organization is not concerned with receiving feedback from former customers, potential customers, and customers of competitors and using feedback information to gauge product/service satisfaction to identify customer support issues and to improve sustainability efforts.

World-Class Organization

- Organization conducts focus groups with former customers, potential customers, and customers of competitors. Data and information is used to gauge their overall concerns with product/services, customer support, and corporate sustainability efforts.
- Organization surveys all former customers, potential customers, and customers of competitors to gauge to what extent sustainability initiatives are important to them in purchasing products/services. Data and information are used to improve the organization's overall sustainability efforts.

☐ Approach   ☐ Deployment   ☐ Learning   ☐ Integration

3.2a(2) The organization listens to former customers, potential customers, and customers of competitors to obtain feedback on products, customer support, transactions, and sustainability efforts.

+ Strengths
1.
2.
3.

– Opportunities for Improvement
1.
2.
3.

Corporate Sustainability Planning Issues:
Economic
1.
2.
Environmental
1.
2.
Social
1.
2.

3.2a(3)   How does your organization manage sustainability complaints?

Interview notes:

Zero-Based Preparation   World-Class Preparation

| 0 | 10 | 20 | 30 | 40 | 50 | 60 | 70 | 80 | 90 | 100 |

| Launching | Evolving | Progressing | Accomplishing | Notable |

(Circle Appropriate Percentile)

Zero-Based Organization

- Organization does not have a dedicated 24-hour mechanism in place to address customer's requests, concerns, and complaints regarding corporate sustainability initiatives.
- Organization does not have a process in place for customers to seek sustainability information, conduct business regarding sustainability issues, and register sustainability complaints.

World-Class Organization

- Organization has a 24-hour, 1-800 phone line and help desk to address corporate sustainability issues and complaints. In addition, a Chief Sustainability Officer (CSO) is in place to address customer concerns.
- Organization has a customer Web site devoted to corporate sustainability. The website allows customers to seek information, conduct business, and register complaints regarding sustainability issues and concerns, 24/7. All complaints are responded to within 12 hours.

☐ Approach   ☐ Deployment   ☐ Learning   ☐ Integration

3.2a(3)   The organization manages sustainability complaints.

+ Strengths

1.
2.
3.

– Opportunities for Improvement

1.
2.
3.

Corporate Sustainability Planning Issues:

Economic

1.
2.

Environmental

1.
2.

Social

1.
2.

3.2b(1)   How does your organization determine customer satisfaction and engagement regarding corporate sustainability efforts?

Interview notes:

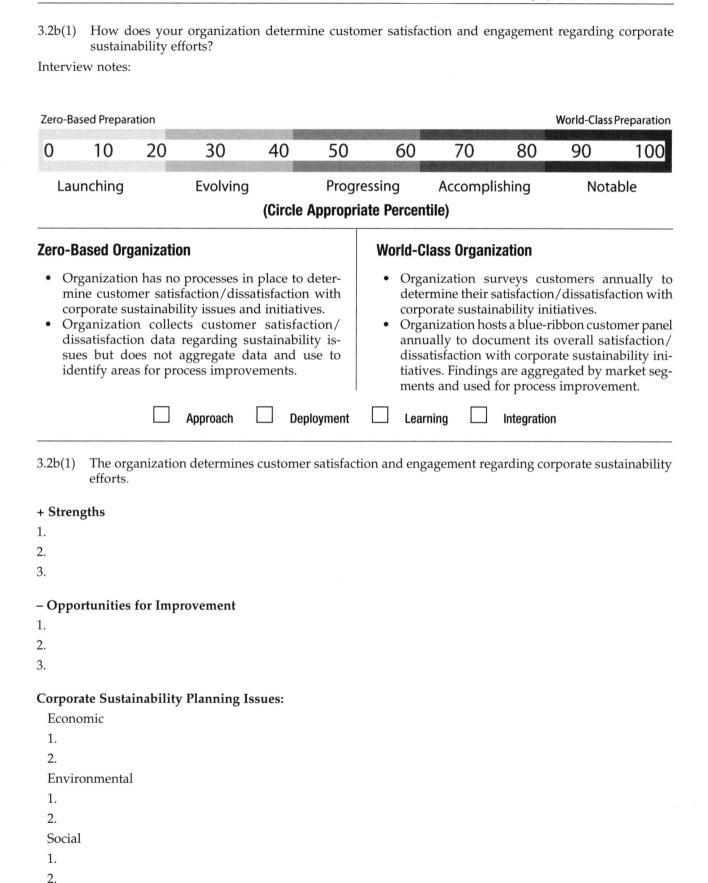

Zero-Based Preparation   World-Class Preparation

| 0 | 10 | 20 | 30 | 40 | 50 | 60 | 70 | 80 | 90 | 100 |

Launching   Evolving   Progressing   Accomplishing   Notable

(Circle Appropriate Percentile)

Zero-Based Organization

- Organization has no processes in place to determine customer satisfaction/dissatisfaction with corporate sustainability issues and initiatives.
- Organization collects customer satisfaction/dissatisfaction data regarding sustainability issues but does not aggregate data and use to identify areas for process improvements.

World-Class Organization

- Organization surveys customers annually to determine their satisfaction/dissatisfaction with corporate sustainability initiatives.
- Organization hosts a blue-ribbon customer panel annually to document its overall satisfaction/dissatisfaction with corporate sustainability initiatives. Findings are aggregated by market segments and used for process improvement.

☐ Approach   ☐ Deployment   ☐ Learning   ☐ Integration

3.2b(1)   The organization determines customer satisfaction and engagement regarding corporate sustainability efforts.

+ Strengths

1.

2.

3.

– Opportunities for Improvement

1.

2.

3.

Corporate Sustainability Planning Issues:

Economic

1.

2.

Environmental

1.

2.

Social

1.

2.

3.2b(2)   How does your organization obtain and use customer satisfaction with corporate sustainability efforts relative to their satisfaction with competitors?

Interview notes:

Zero-Based Preparation   World-Class Preparation

| 0 | 10 | 20 | 30 | 40 | 50 | 60 | 70 | 80 | 90 | 100 |

Launching   Evolving   Progressing   Accomplishing   Notable

(Circle Appropriate Percentile)

Zero-Based Organization

- Organization does not use comparison and benchmark data to gauge customer satisfaction with the organization's sustainability initiatives.
- Organization's data comparisons regarding customer satisfaction with sustainability initiatives relative to the organization's competition appear anecdotal.

World-Class Organization

- Organization uses benchmark and comparison data to improve its sustainability initiatives with customers.
- Organization conducts quarterly satisfaction surveys with key customers to gauge their satisfaction with corporate sustainability efforts relative to their satisfaction with competitors.

☐ Approach   ☐ Deployment   ☐ Learning   ☐ Integration

3.2b(2)   The organization obtains and uses customer satisfaction with corporate sustainability efforts relative to their satisfaction with competitors.

+ Strengths

1.

2.

3.

– Opportunities for Improvement

1.

2.

3.

Corporate Sustainability Planning Issues:

Economic

1.

2.

Environmental

1.

2.

Social

1.

2.

3.2b(3)   How does your organization determine customer dissatisfaction with corporate sustainability efforts?

Interview notes:

Zero-Based Preparation   World-Class Preparation

| 0 | 10 | 20 | 30 | 40 | 50 | 60 | 70 | 80 | 90 | 100 |

Launching   Evolving   Progressing   Accomplishing   Notable

(Circle Appropriate Percentile)

Zero-Based Organization

- Organization has no process in place to determine if customer satisfaction with the organization's approach regarding corporate sustainability issues and initiatives is current and addresses their sustainability needs and directions.
- Organization is not concerned with gauging the currency of its approach to determine customer satisfaction with their corporate sustainability needs and directions.

World-Class Organization

- Organization conducts periodic customer surveys to ensure that corporate sustainability initiatives offered to customers are current with their sustainability needs and directions.
- Customer focus groups are conducted biannually to ensure that the organization's approaches for determining customer satisfaction with sustainability needs and directions are current.

☐ **Approach**   ☐ **Deployment**   ☐ **Learning**   ☐ **Integration**

3.2b(3)   The organization determines customer dissatisfaction with corporate sustainability efforts.

+ Strengths

1.

2.

3.

– Opportunities for Improvement

1.

2.

3.

Corporate Sustainability Planning Issues:

Economic

1.

2.

Environmental

1.

2.

Social

1.

2.

3.2c(1)   How does your organization use customer, market, and product offering information to identify current and anticipate future customer groups and market segments interested in sustainability efforts?

Interview notes:

Zero-Based Preparation   World-Class Preparation

| 0 | 10 | 20 | 30 | 40 | 50 | 60 | 70 | 80 | 90 | 100 |

| Launching | Evolving | Progressing | Accomplishing | Notable |

(Circle Appropriate Percentile)

Zero-Based Organization

- Organization does not have a process in place to obtain information from customers and market segments to gauge their interests in corporate sustainability efforts and initiatives.
- Organization has no interest in gauging customer interest in corporate sustainability efforts.

World-Class Organization

- Organization surveys key customer groups and conducts focus groups and community forums to identify customers and market segments interested in sustainability efforts.
- Organization has developed a corporate sustainability plan based on customer and market survey results and product/service offering information.

☐ Approach   ☐ Deployment   ☐ Learning   ☐ Integration

3.2c(1)   The organization uses customer, market, and product offering information to identify current and anticipate future customer groups and market segments interested in sustainability efforts.

+ Strengths

1.

2.

3.

– Opportunities for Improvement

1.

2.

3.

Corporate Sustainability Planning Issues:

Economic

1.

2.

Environmental

1.

2.

Social

1.

2.

3.2c(2)   How does your organization use customer, market, and product/service offering information to identify and anticipate key customer sustainability requirements, changing sustainability expectations, relative importance of sustainability for purchasing decisions?

Interview notes:

Zero-Based Preparation   World-Class Preparation

| 0 | 10 | 20 | 30 | 40 | 50 | 60 | 70 | 80 | 90 | 100 |

Launching   Evolving   Progressing   Accomplishing   Notable

(Circle Appropriate Percentile)

Zero-Based Organization

- Organization does not use customer market and product/service offering information to identify purchasing decisions based on corporate sustainability efforts.
- Organization has no interest in using sustainability efforts to help customers make increased purchasing decisions.

World-Class Organization

- Organization addresses customer, market, and product/service offering data and information in its corporate sustainability plan to increase customer purchasing decisions.
- Organization incorporates customer, market, and product/service offering information to identify key corporate sustainability initiatives to be considered in the corporate sustainability plan.

☐ Approach   ☐ Deployment   ☐ Learning   ☐ Integration

3.2c(2)   The organization uses customer, market, and product/service offering information to identify sustainability purchasing decisions among customer groups and markets.

+ Strengths
1.
2.
3.

– Opportunities for Improvement
1.
2.
3.

Corporate Sustainability Planning Issues:
Economic
1.
2.
Environmental
1.
2.
Social
1.
2.

3.2c(3)   How does your organization use customer, market, and product/service offering sustainability information to improve marketing, build a more customer-focused culture, and identify opportunities for innovation?

Interview notes:

Zero-Based Preparation   World-Class Preparation

| 0 | 10 | 20 | 30 | 40 | 50 | 60 | 70 | 80 | 90 | 100 |

Launching   Evolving   Progressing   Accomplishing   Notable

(Circle Appropriate Percentile)

Zero-Based Organization	**World-Class Organization**
• Organization does not use customer, market, and product/service offering information to identify innovative sustainability efforts to improve customer service and purchases. • Organization does not consider using customer, market, and product/service offering information to gauge what impact the organization's sustainability efforts are having on customer satisfaction and increased purchases.	• Organization uses customer, market, and product/service offering information on sustainability to better understand factors that drive the organization's markets and affect its competitiveness in product/service offerings. • Organization incorporates customer, market, and product/service offering information to identify innovative opportunities to increase sales based on its sustainability efforts.

☐ Approach   ☐ Deployment   ☐ Learning   ☐ Integration

3.2c(3)   The organization uses customer, market, and product/service offering sustainability information to improve marketing, build a more customer-focused culture, and identify opportunities for innovation.

+ Strengths
1.
2.
3.

– Opportunities for Improvement
1.
2.
3.

Corporate Sustainability Planning Issues:
Economic
1.
2.
Environmental
1.
2.
Social
1.
2.

3.2c(4)   How does your organization keep approaches for customer listening, determination of customer satisfaction/dissatisfaction, and use of customer data current with sustainability needs and directions?

Interview notes:

Zero-Based Preparation   World-Class Preparation

| 0 | 10 | 20 | 30 | 40 | 50 | 60 | 70 | 80 | 90 | 100 |

Launching   Evolving   Progressing   Accomplishing   Notable

(Circle Appropriate Percentile)

Zero-Based Organization

- Organization does not review customer satisfaction/ dissatisfaction data to gauge to what extent it is current with corporate sustainability needs and directions.
- Organization does not use customer data and information to determine current and future directions for corporate sustainability.

World-Class Organization

- Organization uses customer data and listening posts to ensure that its corporate sustainability efforts are current and helping to drive customer satisfaction and loyalty.
- Organization uses its Web site to receive customer input and to ensure that all corporate sustainability efforts are current and meeting and/or exceeding customer expectations and concerns.

☐ Approach   ☐ Deployment   ☐ Learning   ☐ Integration

3.2c(4)   The organization keeps approaches for customer listening, determination of customer satisfaction/ dissatisfaction, and use of customer data current with sustainability needs and directions.

+ Strengths

1.

2.

3.

– Opportunities for Improvement

1.

2.

3.

Corporate Sustainability Planning Issues:

Economic

1.

2.

Environmental

1.

2.

Social

1.

2.

NOTES

6 Category 4: Measurement, Analysis, and Knowledge Management

4 Measurement, Analysis, and Knowledge Management (90 pts.)[14]

The *Measurement, Analysis, and Knowledge Management* Category examines how your organization selects, gathers, analyzes, manages, and improves its data, information, and knowledge assets and how it manages its information technology that is related to corporate sustainability. The Category also examines how your organization reviews, and uses reviews to improve, its overall corporate sustainability performance.

Forms can be downloaded from the CD-ROM located inside the back cover of this book.

4.1 Measurement, Analysis, and Improvement of Organizational Performance (45 pts.)

PROCESS

Describe how your organization measures, analyzes, reviews, and improves its performance through the use of data and information at all levels and in all parts of your organization.

QUESTIONS TO ADDRESS

4.1a(1) How does your organization select, collect, align, and integrate data and information for tracking operations and corporate sustainability initiatives?

4.1a(2) How does your organization select and ensure the effective use of key sustainability comparative data and information to support operational and strategic decision making and innovation?

4.1a(3) How does your organization keep its performance measurement system for corporate sustainability current with business needs and directions?

4.1b How does your organization review corporate sustainability performance and capabilities?

4.1c How does your organization translate organizational performance review findings into priorities for continuous and breakthrough improvement and into opportunities for innovation regarding corporate sustainability?

4.1 Percent Score

☐ Approach   ☐ Deployment   ☐ Learning   ☐ Integration

4.1a(1)   How does your organization select, collect, align, and integrate data and information for tracking operations and corporate sustainability initiatives?

Interview notes:

Zero-Based Preparation   World-Class Preparation

| 0 | 10 | 20 | 30 | 40 | 50 | 60 | 70 | 80 | 90 | 100 |

Launching   Evolving   Progressing   Accomplishing   Notable

(Circle Appropriate Percentile)

Zero-Based Organization

- Organization has no formal selection process in place for information and data to support the organization's corporate sustainability processes, strategic action plans, and performance management systems.
- Organization anecdotally selects and uses sustainability information and data to track overall performance of corporate sustainability initiatives.

World-Class Organization

- Organization has a documented process for the selection, collection, alignment, and tracking of the organization's corporate sustainability data and information.
- Organization has all corporate sustainability information filed and aligned with the Dow Jones Sustainability Index (DJSI) and uses the Index to track corporate-wide sustainability efforts.

☐ Approach   ☐ Deployment   ☐ Learning   ☐ Integration

4.1a(1)   The organization selects, collects, aligns, and integrates data and information for tracking corporate sustainability initiatives.

+ Strengths
1.
2.
3.

– Opportunities for Improvement
1.
2.
3.

Corporate Sustainability Planning Issues:
Economic
1.
2.
Environmental
1.
2.
Social
1.
2.

4.1a(2)   How does your organization select and ensure the effective use of key sustainability comparative data and information to support operational and strategic decision making and innovation?

Interview notes:

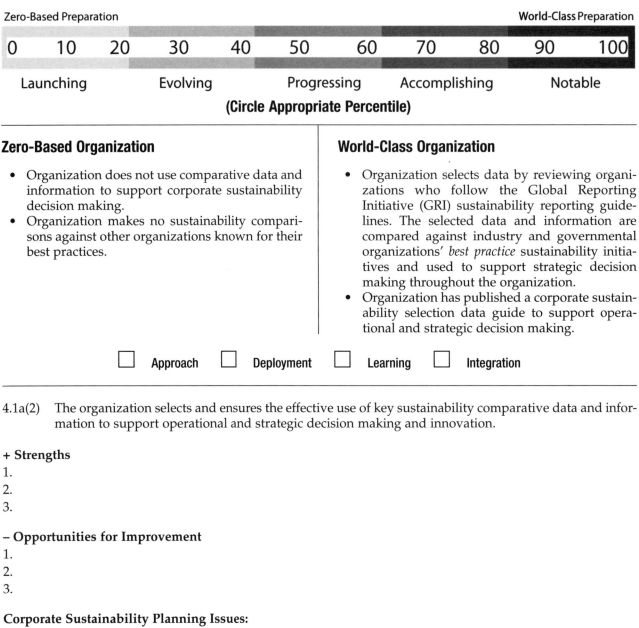

Zero-Based Preparation   World-Class Preparation

| 0 | 10 | 20 | 30 | 40 | 50 | 60 | 70 | 80 | 90 | 100 |

Launching   Evolving   Progressing   Accomplishing   Notable

(Circle Appropriate Percentile)

Zero-Based Organization

- Organization does not use comparative data and information to support corporate sustainability decision making.
- Organization makes no sustainability comparisons against other organizations known for their best practices.

World-Class Organization

- Organization selects data by reviewing organizations who follow the Global Reporting Initiative (GRI) sustainability reporting guidelines. The selected data and information are compared against industry and governmental organizations' *best practice* sustainability initiatives and used to support strategic decision making throughout the organization.
- Organization has published a corporate sustainability selection data guide to support operational and strategic decision making.

☐ Approach   ☐ Deployment   ☐ Learning   ☐ Integration

4.1a(2)   The organization selects and ensures the effective use of key sustainability comparative data and information to support operational and strategic decision making and innovation.

+ Strengths
1.
2.
3.

– Opportunities for Improvement
1.
2.
3.

Corporate Sustainability Planning Issues:
Economic
1.
2.
Environmental
1.
2.
Social
1.
2.

4.1a(3)   How does your organization keep its performance measurement system for corporate sustainability current with business needs and directions?

Interview notes:

Zero-Based Preparation   World-Class Preparation

| 0 | 10 | 20 | 30 | 40 | 50 | 60 | 70 | 80 | 90 | 100 |

Launching   Evolving   Progressing   Accomplishing   Notable

(Circle Appropriate Percentile)

Zero-Based Organization

- Organization does nothing to keep its performance measurement system for corporate sustainability current with business needs and directions.
- Organization has no process in place to ensure that its performance measurement system for corporate sustainability is timely and sensitive to unexpected external environmental, financial, and/or social changes.

World-Class Organization

- Organization reviews its performance measurement system for corporate sustainability annually to ensure it remains current with business needs and directions.
- Organization ensures that its performance measurement system for corporate sustainability is sensitive to rapid and unexpected environmental, financial, and social changes.

☐ Approach   ☐ Deployment   ☐ Learning   ☐ Integration

4.1a(3)   The organization's performance measurement system for corporate sustainability is kept current with business needs and directions.

+ Strengths
1.
2.
3.

– Opportunities for Improvement
1.
2.
3.

Corporate Sustainability Planning Issues:
Economic
1.
2.
Environmental
1.
2.
Social
1.
2.

4.1b   How does your organization review corporate sustainability performance and capabilities?

Interview notes:

Zero-Based Preparation   World-Class Preparation

| 0 | 10 | 20 | 30 | 40 | 50 | 60 | 70 | 80 | 90 | 100 |

Launching   Evolving   Progressing   Accomplishing   Notable

(Circle Appropriate Percentile)

Zero-Based Organization

- Organization uses anecdotal data to support organizational reviews of key corporate sustainability performance and capabilities.
- Organization does not analyze data and information to support performance and capability review of corporate sustainability.

World-Class Organization

- Organization uses *best practice* benchmark data and information to support organizational performance and capability reviews for key corporate sustainability initiatives.
- Organization has developed service quality indicators (SQIs) for key corporate sustainability initiatives and reviews the indicators on a monthly basis to gauge performance and capability.

☐ Approach   ☐ Deployment   ☐ Learning   ☐ Integration

4.1b   The organization reviews corporate sustainability performance and capability.

+ Strengths

1.

2.

3.

– Opportunities for Improvement

1.

2.

3.

Corporate Sustainability Planning Issues:

Economic

1.

2.

Environmental

1.

2.

Social

1.

2.

4.1c How does your organization translate organizational performance review findings into priorities for continuous and breakthrough improvement and into opportunities for innovation regarding corporate sustainability?

Interview notes:

Zero-Based Preparation   World-Class Preparation

| 0 | 10 | 20 | 30 | 40 | 50 | 60 | 70 | 80 | 90 | 100 |

Launching   Evolving   Progressing   Accomplishing   Notable

(Circle Appropriate Percentile)

Zero-Based Organization

- Organization's corporate sustainability data are neither linked to nor supportive of work-group and functional-level decision making regarding corporate sustainability issues.
- Organization does not communicate corporate sustainability data to employees, suppliers, partners, and customers.

World-Class Organization

- Organization's corporate sustainability data is user-friendly and presented in vivid graphs and charts to support functional-level decision making regarding sustainability issues.
- Organization communicates organizational results through its online newsletters to employees, suppliers, partners, and customers. The newsletters are provided to promote breakthrough thinking and improvement in corporate sustainability efforts.

☐ Approach   ☐ Deployment   ☐ Learning   ☐ Integration

4.1c The organization translates organizational performance review findings into priorities for continuous and breakthrough improvement and into opportunities for innovation regarding corporate sustainability.

+ Strengths
1.
2.
3.

– Opportunities for Improvement
1.
2.
3.

Corporate Sustainability Planning Issues:
Economic
1.
2.
Environmental
1.
2.
Social
1.
2.

4.2 Management of Information, Knowledge, and Information Technology (45 pts.)

Describe how your organization ensures the quality and availability of needed data, information, software, and hardware for your workforce, suppliers, partners, collaborators, and customers. Describe how your organization builds and manages its knowledge assets.

QUESTIONS TO ADDRESS

4.2(a)1 How does your organization ensure that its corporate sustainability data, information, and knowledge are accurate, have integrity and reliability, and are timely, secure, and confidential?

4.2a(2) How does your organization ensure that needed corporate sustainability data and information is available to your workforce, suppliers, partners, collaborators, and customers?

4.2a(3) How does your organization collect and transfer relevant organizational knowledge and sharing of best practices that relates to corporate sustainability to and from employees, customers, suppliers, partners, and collaborators to use in your strategic planning process?

4.2b(1) How does your organization ensure that hardware and software supporting corporate sustainability is reliable, secure, and user-friendly?

4.2b(2) How does your organization ensure the continued availability of hardware/software systems and the continued availability of corporate sustainability data and information in the event of an emergency?

4.2b(3) How does your organization keep data and information availability mechanisms that support corporate sustainability, including software and hardware systems, current with business needs and directions, and technological changes in your operating environment?

4.2 Percent Score

☐ Approach ☐ Deployment ☐ Learning ☐ Integration

4.2(a)1   How does your organization ensure that its corporate sustainability data, information, and knowledge are accurate, have integrity and reliability, and are timely, secure, and confidential?

Interview notes:

Zero-Based Preparation   World-Class Preparation

| 0 | 10 | 20 | 30 | 40 | 50 | 60 | 70 | 80 | 90 | 100 |

Launching   Evolving   Progressing   Accomplishing   Notable

(Circle Appropriate Percentile)

Zero-Based Organization

- Organization has no process in place to ensure that corporate sustainability data and knowledge management are reliable, protected, timely, and secure.
- Organization has no ongoing systems in place to review and ensure that corporate sustainability data, information, and organizational knowledge are maintained properly.

World-Class Organization

- Organization surveys data users bimonthly to ensure corporate sustainability data and knowledge management have integrity, timeliness, reliability, security, accuracy, and confidentiality.
- Organization's corporate sustainability data, information, and organizational knowledge are reviewed weekly to ensure that it is reliable, protected, timely, and secure.

☐ Approach   ☐ Deployment   ☐ Learning   ☐ Integration

4.2a(1)   The organization ensures that its corporate sustainability data, information, and knowledge are accurate, have integrity and reliability, and are secure and confidential.

+ Strengths

1.

2.

3.

– Opportunities for Improvement

1.

2.

3.

Corporate Sustainability Planning Issues:

Economic

1.

2.

Environmental

1.

2.

Social

1.

2.

4.2a(2)   How does your organization ensure that needed corporate sustainability data and information are available to your workforce, suppliers, partners, collaborators, and customers?

Interview notes:

Zero-Based Preparation   World-Class Preparation

| 0 | 10 | 20 | 30 | 40 | 50 | 60 | 70 | 80 | 90 | 100 |

| Launching | Evolving | Progressing | Accomplishing | Notable |

(Circle Appropriate Percentile)

Zero-Based Organization

- Organization does not have a consistent and reliable method for deploying corporate sustainability data and information to various stakeholders.
- Organization sends corporate sustainability data and information on a *request only* basis to employees, suppliers, partners, and customers.

World-Class Organization

- Organization uses a subscriber Web site to deploy needed corporate sustainability data and information to their workforce, suppliers, partners, collaborators, and customers.
- Organization has a dedicated corporate sustainability team to dispense needed sustainability data and information to suppliers, partners, and customers daily.

☐ Approach   ☐ Deployment   ☐ Learning   ☐ Integration

4.2a(2)   The organization ensures that needed corporate sustainability data and information is available to the workforce, suppliers, partners, collaborators, and customers.

+ Strengths

1.
2.
3.

– Opportunities for Improvement

1.
2.
3.

Corporate Sustainability Planning Issues:

Economic
1.
2.
Environmental
1.
2.
Social
1.
2.

4.2a(3)   How does your organization collect and transfer relevant organizational knowledge and sharing of best practices that relate to corporate sustainability to and from employees, customers, suppliers, partners, and collaborators to use in your strategic planning process?

Interview notes:

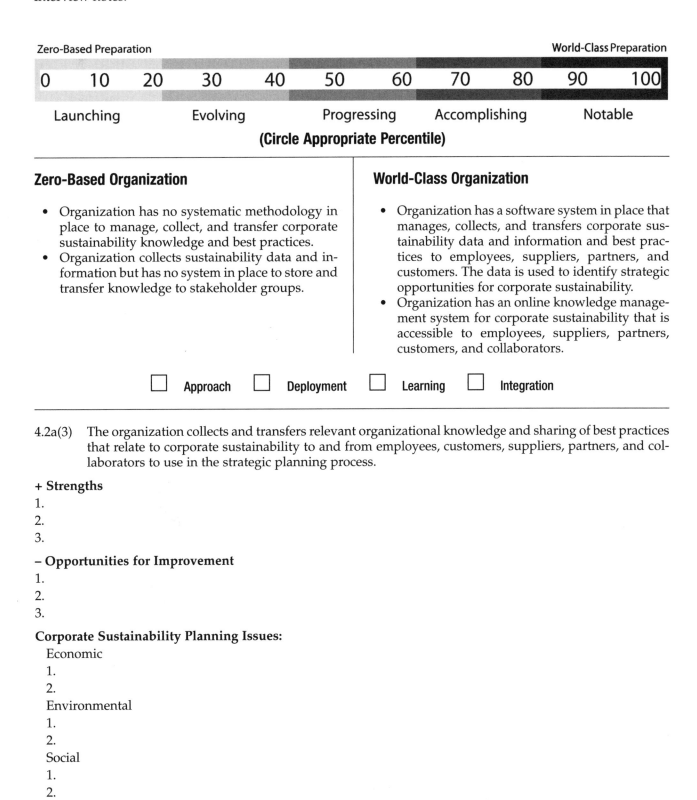

Zero-Based Preparation   World-Class Preparation

| 0 | 10 | 20 | 30 | 40 | 50 | 60 | 70 | 80 | 90 | 100 |

Launching   Evolving   Progressing   Accomplishing   Notable

(Circle Appropriate Percentile)

Zero-Based Organization

- Organization has no systematic methodology in place to manage, collect, and transfer corporate sustainability knowledge and best practices.
- Organization collects sustainability data and information but has no system in place to store and transfer knowledge to stakeholder groups.

World-Class Organization

- Organization has a software system in place that manages, collects, and transfers corporate sustainability data and information and best practices to employees, suppliers, partners, and customers. The data is used to identify strategic opportunities for corporate sustainability.
- Organization has an online knowledge management system for corporate sustainability that is accessible to employees, suppliers, partners, customers, and collaborators.

☐ Approach   ☐ Deployment   ☐ Learning   ☐ Integration

4.2a(3)   The organization collects and transfers relevant organizational knowledge and sharing of best practices that relate to corporate sustainability to and from employees, customers, suppliers, partners, and collaborators to use in the strategic planning process.

+ Strengths
1.
2.
3.

– Opportunities for Improvement
1.
2.
3.

Corporate Sustainability Planning Issues:
Economic
1.
2.
Environmental
1.
2.
Social
1.
2.

4.2b(1) How does your organization ensure that hardware and software supporting corporate sustainability is reliable, secure, and user-friendly?

Interview notes:

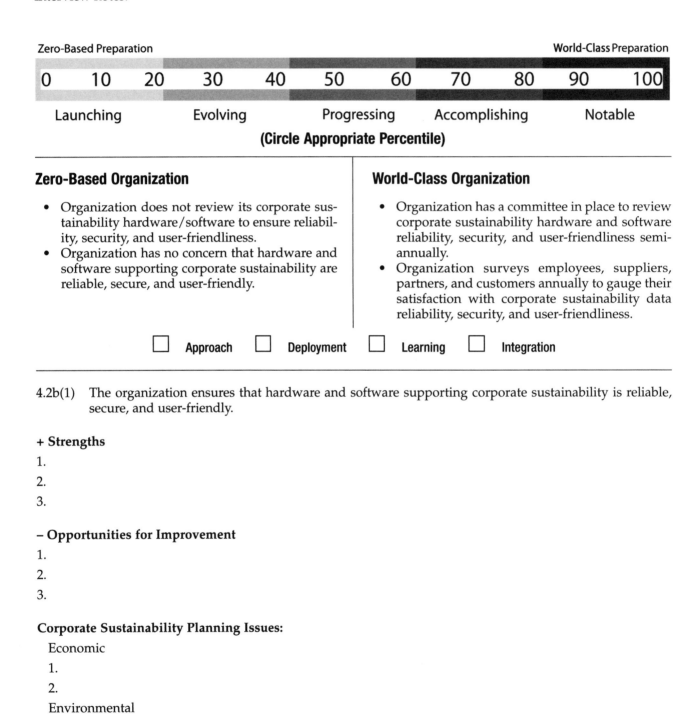

Zero-Based Preparation | World-Class Preparation

| 0 | 10 | 20 | 30 | 40 | 50 | 60 | 70 | 80 | 90 | 100 |

Launching   Evolving   Progressing   Accomplishing   Notable

(Circle Appropriate Percentile)

Zero-Based Organization

- Organization does not review its corporate sustainability hardware/software to ensure reliability, security, and user-friendliness.
- Organization has no concern that hardware and software supporting corporate sustainability are reliable, secure, and user-friendly.

World-Class Organization

- Organization has a committee in place to review corporate sustainability hardware and software reliability, security, and user-friendliness semi-annually.
- Organization surveys employees, suppliers, partners, and customers annually to gauge their satisfaction with corporate sustainability data reliability, security, and user-friendliness.

☐ Approach   ☐ Deployment   ☐ Learning   ☐ Integration

4.2b(1) The organization ensures that hardware and software supporting corporate sustainability is reliable, secure, and user-friendly.

+ Strengths

1.

2.

3.

– Opportunities for Improvement

1.

2.

3.

Corporate Sustainability Planning Issues:

Economic

1.

2.

Environmental

1.

2.

Social

1.

2.

4.2b(2) How does your organization ensure the continued availability of hardware/software systems and the continued availability of corporate sustainability data and information in the event of an emergency?

Interview notes:

            World-Class Preparation

| 0 | 10 | 20 | 30 | 40 | 50 | 60 | 70 | 80 | 90 | 100 |

| Launching | Evolving | Progressing | Accomplishing | Notable |

(Circle Appropriate Percentile)

Zero-Based Organization

- Organization has no formal process in place to ensure hardware/software availability of corporate sustainability data and information in the event of an emergency.
- Organization has no concern for protecting corporate sustainability data and information in the event of an emergency.

World-Class Organization

- Organization has a formal business continuity plan in place that addresses the off-site protection of corporate sustainability data and information in the event of an emergency.
- Organization has developed a Web site for all corporate sustainability data and information that is password-protected and can be accessed by the workforce, key customers, suppliers, and collaborators in the event of an emergency.

☐ Approach   ☐ Deployment   ☐ Learning   ☐ Integration

4.2b(2) The organization ensures the continued availability of hardware/software systems and the continued availability of corporate sustainability data and information in the event of an emergency.

+ Strengths

1.
2.
3.

– Opportunities for Improvement

1.
2.
3.

Corporate Sustainability Planning Issues:

Economic

1.
2.

Environmental

1.
2.

Social

1.
2.

4.2b(3) How does your organization keep data and information availability mechanisms that support corporate sustainability, including software and hardware systems, current with business needs and directions, as well as technological changes in your operating environment?

Interview notes:

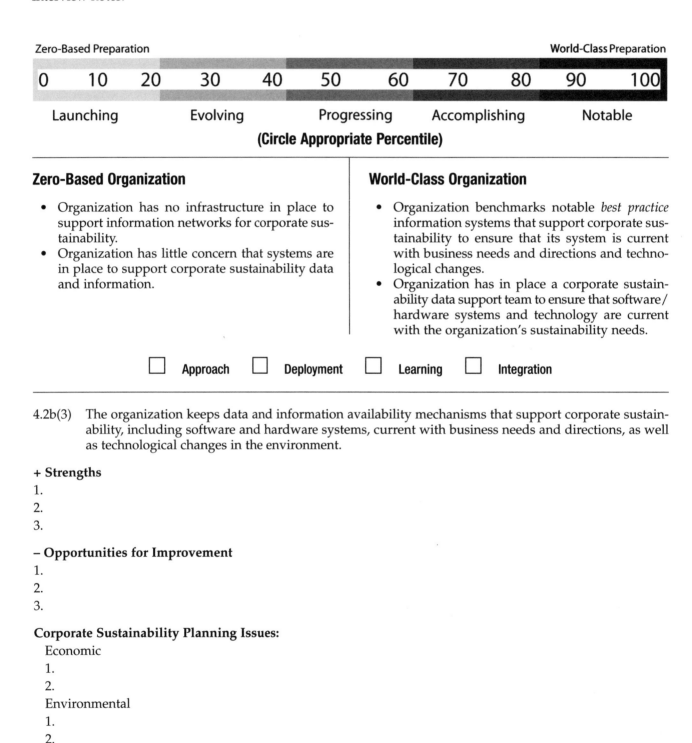

Zero-Based Preparation World-Class Preparation

| 0 | 10 | 20 | 30 | 40 | 50 | 60 | 70 | 80 | 90 | 100 |

Launching Evolving Progressing Accomplishing Notable

(Circle Appropriate Percentile)

Zero-Based Organization

- Organization has no infrastructure in place to support information networks for corporate sustainability.
- Organization has little concern that systems are in place to support corporate sustainability data and information.

World-Class Organization

- Organization benchmarks notable *best practice* information systems that support corporate sustainability to ensure that its system is current with business needs and directions and technological changes.
- Organization has in place a corporate sustainability data support team to ensure that software/hardware systems and technology are current with the organization's sustainability needs.

☐ Approach ☐ Deployment ☐ Learning ☐ Integration

4.2b(3) The organization keeps data and information availability mechanisms that support corporate sustainability, including software and hardware systems, current with business needs and directions, as well as technological changes in the environment.

+ Strengths
1.
2.
3.

– Opportunities for Improvement
1.
2.
3.

Corporate Sustainability Planning Issues:
Economic
1.
2.
Environmental
1.
2.
Social
1.
2.

NOTES

7

Category 5
Workforce Focus

5 Workforce Focus (85 pts.)[15]

The *Workforce Focus* Category examines how your organization engages, manages, and develops your workforce to utilize its full potential in alignment with your organization's overall mission, strategy, and action plans that relate to corporate sustainability. The Category examines your ability to assess workforce capability and capacity needs and to build a workforce environment conducive to high performance and corporate sustainability.

 Forms can be downloaded from the CD-ROM located inside the back cover of this book.

5.1 Workforce Engagement (45 pts.)

Describe how your organization engages, compensates, and rewards your workforce to achieve high performance. Describe how members of your workforce, including leaders, are developed to achieve high performance. Describe how you assess workforce engagement and use the results to achieve higher performance.

QUESTIONS TO ADDRESS

5.1a(1) How does your organization determine key factors that affect workforce engagement in corporate sustainability issues?

5.1a(2) How does your organization's culture promote open communication, high performance work, and an engaged workforce that benefits from diverse ideas, cultures, and thinking that is related to corporate sustainability?

5.1a(3) How does your organization's workforce performance management system support corporate sustainability initiatives within the organization and reward, recognize, and compensate the workforce for reinforcing a customer and business focus and achievement of your action plans?

5.1b(1) How does your organization's learning and development system address core competencies, strategic challenges, accomplishment of its action plans, performance improvement, innovation, ethics, training, coaching, mentoring, and work-related experiences as they relate to corporate sustainability?

5.1b(2) How does your organization's workforce learning and development system address transfer of knowledge from departing or retiring workers and reinforce new knowledge and skills on the job as they relate to corporate sustainability?

5.1b(3) How does your organization evaluate the effectiveness and efficiency of corporate sustainability learning and development systems?

5.1b(4) How does your organization manage effective career progression and accomplish effective succession planning for management and leadership positions as it relates to corporate sustainability for the entire workforce?

5.1c(1) How does your organization assess workforce engagement as it relates to corporate sustainability?

5.1c(2) How does your organization relate workforce engagement assessment findings to key corporate sustainability and business results?

5.1 Percent Score

☐ Approach   ☐ Deployment   ☐ Learning   ☐ Integration

5.1a(1)   How does your organization determine key factors that affect workforce engagement in corporate sustainability issues?

Interview notes:

Zero-Based Preparation   World-Class Preparation

| 0 | 10 | 20 | 30 | 40 | 50 | 60 | 70 | 80 | 90 | 100 |

Launching   Evolving   Progressing   Accomplishing   Notable

(Circle Appropriate Percentile)

Zero-Based Organization	World-Class Organization
• Organization offers limited opportunities for workers to be engaged in corporate sustainability issues. • Organization does not allow employees to review and discuss sustainability issues on company time. Workers are disciplined who engage in environmental, societal, and labor-related issues.	• Organization recognizes and rewards the workforce for working in cross-functional problem solving teams to address and ultimately help solve corporate sustainability issues that affect the environment, society, and economic concerns that impact the organization. • Organization rewards workers who are engaged in corporate sustainability issues with a year-end bonus plan.

☐ **Approach**   ☐ **Deployment**   ☐ **Learning**   ☐ **Integration**

5.1a(1)   The organization determines key factors that affect workforce engagement in corporate sustainability issues.

+ Strengths
1.
2.
3.

– Opportunities for Improvement
1.
2.
3.

Corporate Sustainability Planning Issues:
Economic
1.
2.
Environmental
1.
2.
Social
1.
2.

5.1a(2)   How does your organization's culture promote open communication, high performance work, and an engaged workforce that benefits from diverse ideas, cultures, and thinking that is related to corporate sustainability?

Interview notes:

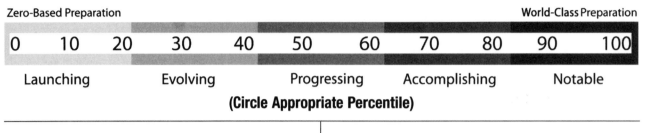

Zero-Based Preparation   World-Class Preparation

| 0 | 10 | 20 | 30 | 40 | 50 | 60 | 70 | 80 | 90 | 100 |

Launching   Evolving   Progressing   Accomplishing   Notable

(Circle Appropriate Percentile)

Zero-Based Organization

- Organization's work systems are not formalized and do not capitalize on diverse thinking among employees regarding corporate sustainability.
- Organization's work systems do not support employee interaction regarding corporate sustainability issues.

World-Class Organization

- Organization's corporate sustainability work teams, process teams, and peer coaching teams encourage high performance and promote diverse ideas and thinking throughout the organization about sustainability issues and vulnerabilities.
- Organization promotes cross-functional teams among employees to capitalize on their diverse ideas, cultures, and diverse thinking to identify corporate sustainability issues and vulnerabilities.

☐ Approach   ☐ Deployment   ☐ Learning   ☐ Integration

5.1a(2)   The organization's culture promotes open communication, high performance work, and an engaged workforce that benefits from diverse ideas, cultures, and thinking that is related to corporate sustainability.

+ Strengths

1.
2.
3.

– Opportunities for Improvement

1.
2.
3.

Corporate Sustainability Planning Issues:

Economic
1.
2.
Environmental
1.
2.
Social
1.
2.

5.1a(3)   How does your organization's workforce performance management system support corporate sustainability initiatives within the organization and reward, recognize, and compensate the workforce for reinforcing a customer and business focus and achievement of your action plans?

Interview notes:

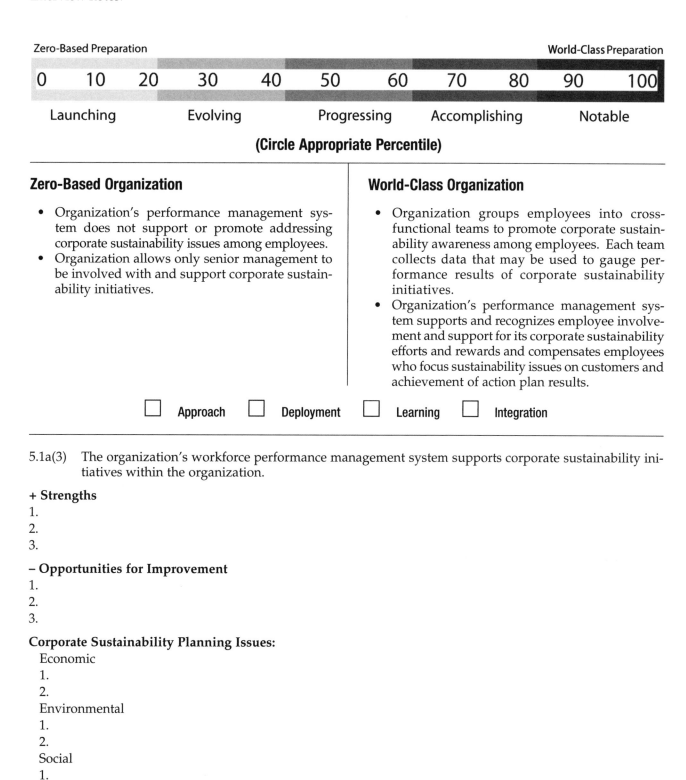

Zero-Based Preparation   World-Class Preparation

| 0 | 10 | 20 | 30 | 40 | 50 | 60 | 70 | 80 | 90 | 100 |

Launching   Evolving   Progressing   Accomplishing   Notable

(Circle Appropriate Percentile)

Zero-Based Organization

- Organization's performance management system does not support or promote addressing corporate sustainability issues among employees.
- Organization allows only senior management to be involved with and support corporate sustainability initiatives.

World-Class Organization

- Organization groups employees into cross-functional teams to promote corporate sustainability awareness among employees. Each team collects data that may be used to gauge performance results of corporate sustainability initiatives.
- Organization's performance management system supports and recognizes employee involvement and support for its corporate sustainability efforts and rewards and compensates employees who focus sustainability issues on customers and achievement of action plan results.

☐ Approach   ☐ Deployment   ☐ Learning   ☐ Integration

5.1a(3)   The organization's workforce performance management system supports corporate sustainability initiatives within the organization.

+ Strengths
1.
2.
3.

– Opportunities for Improvement
1.
2.
3.

Corporate Sustainability Planning Issues:
Economic
1.
2.
Environmental
1.
2.
Social
1.
2.

5.1b(1) How does your organization's learning and development system address core competencies, strategic challenges, accomplishment of its action plans, performance improvement, innovation, ethics, training, coaching, mentoring, and work-related experiences as they relate to corporate sustainability?

Interview notes:

Zero-Based Preparation   World-Class Preparation

| 0 | 10 | 20 | 30 | 40 | 50 | 60 | 70 | 80 | 90 | 100 |

Launching   Evolving   Progressing   Accomplishing   Notable

(Circle Appropriate Percentile)

Zero-Based Organization

- Organization's education and training do not support corporate sustainability strategic goals.
- Organization has limited training that contributes to the achievement of corporate sustainability and helps accomplish strategic challenges, ethics, innovation, and performance improvement action plans.

World-Class Organization

- Organization's employee training and development needs are integrated with its short- and long-term strategic plans and goals that support corporate sustainability.
- Organization's employee workshops and training programs address topics that support its key strategic corporate sustainability goals and action plans.

☐ Approach   ☐ Deployment   ☐ Learning   ☐ Integration

5.1b(1) The organization's learning and development system addresses corporate sustainability.

+ Strengths

1.
2.
3.

– Opportunities for Improvement

1.
2.
3.

Corporate Sustainability Planning Issues:

Economic

1.
2.

Environmental

1.
2.

Social

1.
2.

5.1b(2) How does your organization's workforce learning and development system address transfer of knowledge from departing or retiring workers and reinforce new knowledge and skills on the job as they relate to corporate sustainability?

Interview notes:

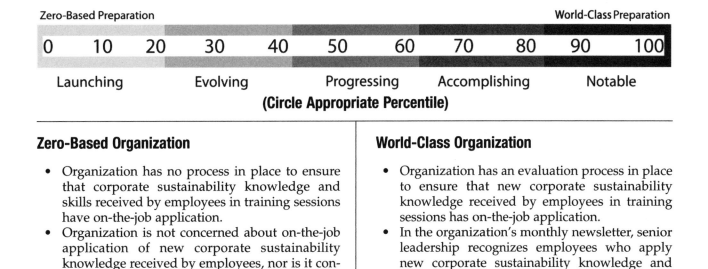

Zero-Based Preparation

World-Class Preparation

| 0 | 10 | 20 | 30 | 40 | 50 | 60 | 70 | 80 | 90 | 100 |

Launching   Evolving   Progressing   Accomplishing   Notable

(Circle Appropriate Percentile)

Zero-Based Organization

- Organization has no process in place to ensure that corporate sustainability knowledge and skills received by employees in training sessions have on-the-job application.
- Organization is not concerned about on-the-job application of new corporate sustainability knowledge received by employees, nor is it concerned with capturing and transferring knowledge from departing or retiring workers.

World-Class Organization

- Organization has an evaluation process in place to ensure that new corporate sustainability knowledge received by employees in training sessions has on-the-job application.
- In the organization's monthly newsletter, senior leadership recognizes employees who apply new corporate sustainability knowledge and skills received through training on the job.

☐ Approach   ☐ Deployment   ☐ Learning   ☐ Integration

5.1b(2) The organization's workforce learning and development system addresses transfer of knowledge from departing or retiring workers and reinforces new knowledge and skills on the job as they relate to corporate sustainability.

+ Strengths
1.
2.
3.

– Opportunities for Improvement
1.
2.
3.

Corporate Sustainability Planning Issues:
Economic
1.
2.
Environmental
1.
2.
Social
1.
2.

5.1b(3)   How does your organization evaluate the effectiveness and efficiency of corporate sustainability learning and development systems?

Interview notes:

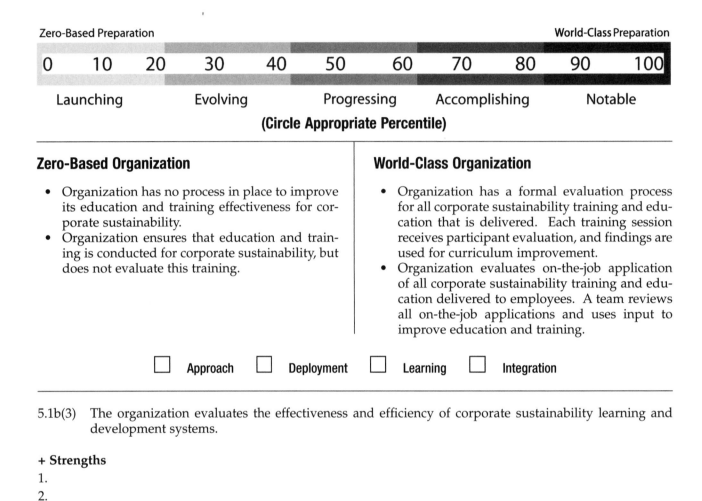

Zero-Based Preparation   World-Class Preparation

| 0 | 10 | 20 | 30 | 40 | 50 | 60 | 70 | 80 | 90 | 100 |

Launching   Evolving   Progressing   Accomplishing   Notable

(Circle Appropriate Percentile)

Zero-Based Organization

- Organization has no process in place to improve its education and training effectiveness for corporate sustainability.
- Organization ensures that education and training is conducted for corporate sustainability, but does not evaluate this training.

World-Class Organization

- Organization has a formal evaluation process for all corporate sustainability training and education that is delivered. Each training session receives participant evaluation, and findings are used for curriculum improvement.
- Organization evaluates on-the-job application of all corporate sustainability training and education delivered to employees. A team reviews all on-the-job applications and uses input to improve education and training.

☐ Approach   ☐ Deployment   ☐ Learning   ☐ Integration

5.1b(3)   The organization evaluates the effectiveness and efficiency of corporate sustainability learning and development systems.

+ Strengths

1.
2.
3.

– Opportunities for Improvement

1.
2.
3.

Corporate Sustainability Planning Issues:

Economic
1.
2.
Environmental
1.
2.
Social
1.
2.

5.1b(4) How does your organization manage effective career progression and accomplish effective succession planning for management and leadership positions as they relate to corporate sustainability for the entire workforce?

Interview notes:

Zero-Based Preparation   World-Class Preparation

| 0 | 10 | 20 | 30 | 40 | 50 | 60 | 70 | 80 | 90 | 100 |

Launching   Evolving   Progressing   Accomplishing   Notable

(Circle Appropriate Percentile)

Zero-Based Organization

- Organization has no processes in place to motivate employees to develop and use their full potential to ensure a sustainable work environment.
- Organization has no concern for motivating employees to develop their knowledge and skills to ensure a sustainable work environment.

World-Class Organization

- Organization has developed a leadership academy for corporate sustainability to motivate employees to attain job- and career-related development and to use their full potential to ensure a sustainable work environment.
- Organization has a formal recognition program in place that motivates and rewards employees to develop and use their full potential in ensuring a sustainable work environment.

☐ Approach   ☐ Deployment   ☐ Learning   ☐ Integration

5.1b(4) The organization manages effective career progression and accomplishes effective succession planning for management and leadership positions as they relate to corporate sustainability for the entire workforce.

+ Strengths
1.
2.
3.

– Opportunities for Improvement
1.
2.
3.

Corporate Sustainability Planning Issues:
Economic
  1.
  2.
Environmental
  1.
  2.
Social
  1.
  2.

5.1c(1)   How does your organization assess workforce engagement as it relates to corporate sustainability?

Interview notes:

Zero-Based Preparation   World-Class Preparation

| 0 | 10 | 20 | 30 | 40 | 50 | 60 | 70 | 80 | 90 | 100 |

Launching   Evolving   Progressing   Accomplishing   Notable

(Circle Appropriate Percentile)

Zero-Based Organization

- Organization conducts very little workforce engagement assessments related to corporate sustainability for employees and has no formal assessment methodology in place.
- Organization conducts informal assessments for corporate sustainability as needed. No systematic design process is in place for the workforce that gauges employee engagement in sustainability initiatives.

World-Class Organization

- Organization has a corporate sustainability engagement team in place that is made up of selected employees and various stakeholders to evaluate workforce engagement initiatives that support overall sustainability needs and objectives.
- Organization identifies and has a design methodology in place to assess workforce engagement in corporate sustainability initiatives.

☐ Approach   ☐ Deployment   ☐ Learning   ☐ Integration

5.1c(1)   The organization assesses workforce engagement as it relates to corporate sustainability.

+ Strengths

1.

2.

3.

- Opportunities for Improvement

1.

2.

3.

Corporate Sustainability Planning Issues:

Economic

1.

2.

Environmental

1.

2.

Social

1.

2.

5.1c(2)   How does your organization relate workforce engagement assessment findings to key corporate sustainability and business results?

Interview notes:

Zero-Based Preparation   World-Class Preparation

| 0 | 10 | 20 | 30 | 40 | 50 | 60 | 70 | 80 | 90 | 100 |

Launching   Evolving   Progressing   Accomplishing   Notable

(Circle Appropriate Percentile)

Zero-Based Organization

- Organization has nothing in place that relates workforce engagement in sustainability issues to their impact on business results.
- Organization does not relate workplace safety and security, diversity, and teamwork assessment findings to key corporate sustainability and business results.

World-Class Organization

- Organization assesses its workforce grievance resolution, career development, safety and security, and teamwork to corporate sustainability and business results on an annual basis.
- Organization uses formal surveys and focus group data and information to assess turnover, grievances, and strikes as they relate to corporate sustainability and business results.

☐ Approach   ☐ Deployment   ☐ Learning   ☐ Integration

5.1c(2)   The organization relates workforce engagement assessment findings to key corporate sustainability and business results.

+ Strengths

1.

2.

3.

– Opportunities for Improvement

1.

2.

3.

Corporate Sustainability Planning Issues:

Economic

1.

2.

Environmental

1.

2.

Social

1.

2.

5.2 Workforce Environment (40 pts.)

Describe how your organization manages workforce capability and capacity to accomplish the work of the organization. Describe how your organization maintains a safe, secure, and supportive work climate.

PROCESS

QUESTIONS TO ADDRESS

5.2a(1)   How does your organization assess your workforce capability and capacity needs, including skills, competencies, and staffing levels for corporate sustainability?

5.2a(2)   How does your organization recruit, hire, place, and retain new members of the workforce to ensure corporate sustainability?

5.2a(3)   How does your organization manage and organize the workforce to accomplish corporate sustainability?

5.2a(4)   How does your organization prepare the workforce for changing capability and capacity needs to ensure corporate sustainability?

5.2b(1)   How does your organization address workplace environmental factors to ensure and improve corporate sustainability and workforce health, safety, and security?

5.2b(2)   How does your organization support a sustainable workforce via policies, services, and benefits?

5.2 Percent Score

☐ Approach   ☐ Deployment   ☐ Learning   ☐ Integration

5.2a(1)   How does your organization assess your workforce capability and capacity needs, including skills, competencies, and staffing levels for corporate sustainability?

Interview notes:

Zero-Based Preparation   World-Class Preparation

| 0 | 10 | 20 | 30 | 40 | 50 | 60 | 70 | 80 | 90 | 100 |

Launching   Evolving   Progressing   Accomplishing   Notable

(Circle Appropriate Percentile)

Zero-Based Organization

- No systematic process is in place to assess work and jobs for employees that promote cooperation, empowerment, innovation, and collaboration, regarding corporate sustainability.
- Organization does not address work system structure that promotes cooperation and collaboration of employees and meets corporate sustainability needs.

World-Class Organization

- Organization conducts an annual work system review to ensure that employees' cooperation and collaboration meet the organization's corporate sustainability capability and capacity needs and goals.
- Employees are grouped into various work teams (for example, safety teams, cross-functional teams) to promote cooperation and collaboration to keep current the organization's corporate sustainability capability and capacity staffing needs and to ensure that workforce skills and competencies are adequate for the organization to meet its strategic goals and plans.

☐ Approach   ☐ Deployment   ☐ Learning   ☐ Integration

5.2a(1)   The organization assesses workforce capability and capacity needs, including skills, competencies, and staffing levels, for corporate sustainability.

+ Strengths
1.
2.
3.

– Opportunities for Improvement
1.
2.
3.

Corporate Sustainability Planning Issues:
Economic
  1.
  2.
Environmental
  1.
  2.
Social
  1.
  2.

5.2a(2) How does your organization recruit, hire, place, and retain new members of the workforce to ensure corporate sustainability?

Interview notes:

Zero-Based Preparation   World-Class Preparation

| 0 | 10 | 20 | 30 | 40 | 50 | 60 | 70 | 80 | 90 | 100 |

Launching   Evolving   Progressing   Accomplishing   Notable

(Circle Appropriate Percentile)

Zero-Based Organization	**World-Class Organization**
• Organization has no consistent corporate sustainability policies or procedures that address recruiting, hiring, and retaining new employees. • Organization has not addressed corporate sustainability issues for potential and newly hired employees.	• Organization has documented procedures in place that address recruiting, hiring, and retaining new employees to ensure a sustainable work environment. • Organization has developed a corporate sustainability orientation program for potential and newly hired employees that promotes a sustainable work environment.

☐ **Approach**   ☐ **Deployment**   ☐ **Learning**   ☐ **Integration**

5.2a(2) The organization recruits, hires, places, and retains new members of the workforce to ensure corporate sustainability.

+ Strengths

1.

2.

3.

– Opportunities for Improvement

1.

2.

3.

Corporate Sustainability Planning Issues:

Economic

1.

2.

Environmental

1.

2.

Social

1.

2.

5.2a(3)   How does your organization manage and organize the workforce to accomplish corporate sustainability?

Interview notes:

Zero-Based Preparation   World-Class Preparation

| 0 | 10 | 20 | 30 | 40 | 50 | 60 | 70 | 80 | 90 | 100 |

Launching   Evolving   Progressing   Accomplishing   Notable

(Circle Appropriate Percentile)

Zero-Based Organization

- Organization has no process in place to ensure effective communication, cooperation, and knowledge/skill sharing among employees regarding corporate sustainability.
- Corporate sustainability knowledge/skill sharing among employees is not encouraged by the organization's leadership.

World-Class Organization

- Organization requires all cross-functional teams to share their corporate sustainability project results on the organization's password protected intranet.
- Organization promotes the use of e-mail and in-house workshops for employees to communicate and share corporate sustainability knowledge and skills organization-wide.

☐ Approach   ☐ Deployment   ☐ Learning   ☐ Integration

5.2a(3)   The organization manages and organizes the workforce to accomplish corporate sustainability.

+ Strengths

1.

2.

3.

– Opportunities for Improvement

1.

2.

3.

Corporate Sustainability Planning Issues:

Economic

1.

2.

Environmental

1.

2.

Social

1.

2.

5.2a(4)   How does your organization prepare the workforce for changing capability and capacity needs to ensure corporate sustainability?

Interview notes:

Zero-Based Preparation   World-Class Preparation

| 0 | 10 | 20 | 30 | 40 | 50 | 60 | 70 | 80 | 90 | 100 |

Launching   Evolving   Progressing   Accomplishing   Notable

(Circle Appropriate Percentile)

Zero-Based Organization

- Organization has nothing in place to build and sustain staff relationships with customers, to develop new sustainable products, services, and work processes, and to meet increasing regulatory demands that promote a sustainable work environment.
- Organization has no well-defined process in place to prepare the workforce for capability changes such as technology enhancements and capacity changes needed to ensure sufficient staffing levels are in place to maintain corporate sustainability.

World-Class Organization

- Organization has formal plans in place to notify employees in advance of any potential workforce reductions to meet seasonal or varying demand levels to ensure corporate sustainability.
- Organization uses forecast reports to anticipate changing capability and capacity workforce needs based on varying customer demand levels to ensure corporate sustainability. The forecast information is shared on a monthly basis with all employee levels.

☐ Approach   ☐ Deployment   ☐ Learning   ☐ Integration

5.2a(4)   The organization prepares the workforce for changing capability and capacity needs to ensure corporate sustainability.

+ Strengths
1.
2.
3.

– Opportunities for Improvement
1.
2.
3.

Corporate Sustainability Planning Issues:
  Economic
  1.
  2.
  Environmental
  1.
  2.
  Social
  1.
  2.

5.2b(1)   How does your organization address workplace environmental factors to ensure and improve corporate sustainability and workforce health, safety, and security?

Interview notes:

Zero-Based Preparation   World-Class Preparation

| 0 | 10 | 20 | 30 | 40 | 50 | 60 | 70 | 80 | 90 | 100 |

Launching   Evolving   Progressing   Accomplishing   Notable

(Circle Appropriate Percentile)

Zero-Based Organization

- Organization does not address workplace environmental factors to ensure corporate sustainability.
- Organization has no concern for environmental factors that ensure and improve corporate sustainability by improving health, safety, and security.

World-Class Organization

- Organization has in place strategic plans and goals that address workforce health, safety, and security issues that will ensure ongoing corporate sustainability.
- Organization has training, education, and monthly employee meetings that address workplace health, safety, and security issues to ensure ongoing corporate sustainability.

☐ Approach   ☐ Deployment   ☐ Learning   ☐ Integration

5.2b(1)   The organization addresses workplace environmental factors to ensure and improve corporate sustainability and workforce health, safety, and security.

+ Strengths
1.
2.
3.

– Opportunities for Improvement
1.
2.
3.

Corporate Sustainability Planning Issues:

Economic
1.
2.
Environmental
1.
2.
Social
1.
2.

5.2b(2)   How does your organization support a sustainable workforce via policies, services, and benefits?

Interview notes:

| 0 | 10 | 20 | 30 | 40 | 50 | 60 | 70 | 80 | 90 | 100 |

Launching   Evolving   Progressing   Accomplishing   Notable

(Circle Appropriate Percentile)

Zero-Based Organization

- Organization does nothing to maintain a safe, secure, and healthful work environment to support a sustainable workforce.
- Organization's leadership has no concern for maintaining an environment that is safe, secure, and healthful and that supports the well-being, satisfaction, and motivation of employees through policies, services, and benefits.

World-Class Organization

- Organization surveys employees to determine to what extent the work environment supports their safety and health. Findings are used to address areas of concern regarding corporate sustainability.
- Organization provides counseling to employees regarding safety, security, and health issues that are related to corporate sustainability. Policies, services, and benefits have been developed to support a sustainable organization.

☐ Approach   ☐ Deployment   ☐ Learning   ☐ Integration

5.2b(2)   The organization supports a sustainable workforce via policies, services, and benefits.

+ Strengths

1.

2.

3.

– Opportunities for Improvement

1.

2.

3.

Corporate Sustainability Planning Issues:

Economic

1.

2.

Environmental

1.

2.

Social

1.

2.

NOTES

8

Category 6: Process Management

6 Process Management (85 pts.)[16]

The *Process Management* Category examines how your organization designs its work systems and how it designs, manages, and improves its key processes for implementing those work systems to deliver customer value and achieve organizational success and sustainability. Also examined is your readiness for emergencies.

Forms can be downloaded from the CD-ROM located inside the back cover of this book.

6.1 Work Systems (35 pts.)

Describe how your organization designs its work systems and determines its key processes to deliver customer value, prepare for potential emergencies, and achieve organizational success and sustainability.

PROCESS

QUESTIONS TO ADDRESS

6.1a(1) How does your organization design and innovate overall work systems related to corporate sustainability?

6.1a(2) How do your organization's work systems and key work processes relate to and capitalize on core corporate sustainability competencies?

6.1b(1) What are your organization's key work processes to ensure corporate sustainability?

6.1b(2) How does your organization determine key work process requirements for corporate sustainability, incorporating input from customers, suppliers, partners, and collaborators?

6.1c How does your organization ensure work systems and workplace preparedness for disasters or emergencies to ensure corporate sustainability?

6.1 Percent Score

☐ Approach   ☐ Deployment   ☐ Learning   ☐ Integration

6.1a(1) How does your organization design and innovate overall work systems related to corporate sustainability?

Interview notes:

Zero-Based Preparation   World-Class Preparation

| 0 | 10 | 20 | 30 | 40 | 50 | 60 | 70 | 80 | 90 | 100 |

Launching   Evolving   Progressing   Accomplishing   Notable

(Circle Appropriate Percentile)

Zero-Based Organization	World-Class Organization
• Organization has no quality control for corporate sustainability processes that have been designed to ensure a sustainable environment. • Organization does not consider stakeholders and their requirements when designing key processes for corporate sustainability.	• Organization conducts assessments to ensure that critical corporate sustainability processes meet design requirements and incorporate cycle time and other efficiency and effectiveness factors into the design of the processes. • Organization's corporate sustainability program designs are reviewed by cross-functional employee and stakeholder teams to ensure that design requirements are being met.

☐ Approach   ☐ Deployment   ☐ Learning   ☐ Integration

6.1a(1) The organization designs and innovates overall work systems related to corporate sustainability.

+ Strengths

1.

2.

3.

– Opportunities for Improvement

1.

2.

3.

Corporate Sustainability Planning Issues:

Economic

1.

2.

Environmental

1.

2.

Social

1.

2.

6.1a(2)   How do your organization's work systems and key work processes relate to and capitalize on core corporate sustainability competencies?

Interview notes:

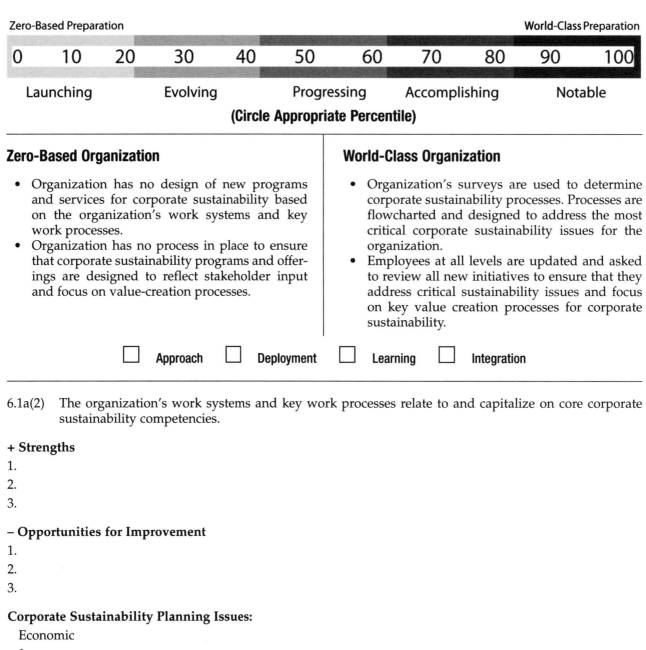

Zero-Based Preparation   World-Class Preparation

| 0 | 10 | 20 | 30 | 40 | 50 | 60 | 70 | 80 | 90 | 100 |

Launching   Evolving   Progressing   Accomplishing   Notable

(Circle Appropriate Percentile)

Zero-Based Organization

- Organization has no design of new programs and services for corporate sustainability based on the organization's work systems and key work processes.
- Organization has no process in place to ensure that corporate sustainability programs and offerings are designed to reflect stakeholder input and focus on value-creation processes.

World-Class Organization

- Organization's surveys are used to determine corporate sustainability processes. Processes are flowcharted and designed to address the most critical corporate sustainability issues for the organization.
- Employees at all levels are updated and asked to review all new initiatives to ensure that they address critical sustainability issues and focus on key value creation processes for corporate sustainability.

☐ Approach   ☐ Deployment   ☐ Learning   ☐ Integration

6.1a(2)   The organization's work systems and key work processes relate to and capitalize on core corporate sustainability competencies.

+ Strengths
1.
2.
3.

− Opportunities for Improvement
1.
2.
3.

Corporate Sustainability Planning Issues:
Economic
1.
2.
Environmental
1.
2.
Social
1.
2.

6.1b(1) What are your organization's key work processes to ensure corporate sustainability?

Interview notes:

Zero-Based Preparation   World-Class Preparation

0	10	20	30	40	50	60	70	80	90	100

Launching   Evolving   Progressing   Accomplishing   Notable

(Circle Appropriate Percentile)

Zero-Based Organization

- Organization does not seek input from stakeholders to determine key processes that support corporate sustainability.
- Organization determines key processes that support corporate sustainability without input from employees and stakeholder groups.

World-Class Organization

- Organization determines its critical processes that support corporate sustainability initiatives based on focus group input from key stakeholder groups.
- Organization surveys employees, suppliers, customers, and partners annually to determine key processes that support corporate sustainability.

☐ Approach   ☐ Deployment   ☐ Learning   ☐ Integration

6.1b(1) The organization has key work processes to ensure corporate sustainability.

+ Strengths
1.
2.
3.

– Opportunities for Improvement
1.
2.
3.

Corporate Sustainability Planning Issues:

Economic
1.
2.

Environmental
1.
2.

Social
1.
2.

6.1b(2)   How does your organization determine key work process requirements for corporate sustainability, incorporating input from customers, suppliers, partners, and collaborators?

Interview notes:

Zero-Based Preparation   World-Class Preparation

| 0 | 10 | 20 | 30 | 40 | 50 | 60 | 70 | 80 | 90 | 100 |

Launching   Evolving   Progressing   Accomplishing   Notable

(Circle Appropriate Percentile)

Zero-Based Organization

- Organization does not use a systematic approach to evaluate and improve key corporate sustainability value creation processes.
- Organization does not include stakeholders to help determine key corporate sustainability value-creation processes.

World-Class Organization

- Organization has a structured evaluation process to ensure that key value-creation processes for corporate sustainability requirements are identified and flowcharted and involve all stakeholder groups.
- Organization incorporates a simple flowchart of key corporate sustainability processes and includes key customers, suppliers, and partners to identify key value-creation processes.

☐ **Approach**   ☐ **Deployment**   ☐ **Learning**   ☐ **Integration**

6.1b(2)   The organization determines key work process requirements for corporate sustainability, incorporating input from customers, suppliers, partners, and collaborators.

+ Strengths

1.
2.
3.

– Opportunities for Improvement

1.
2.
3.

Corporate Sustainability Planning Issues:

Economic
1.
2.
Environmental
1.
2.
Social
1.
2.

6.1c   How does your organization ensure work systems and workplace preparedness for disasters or emergencies to ensure corporate sustainability?

Interview notes:

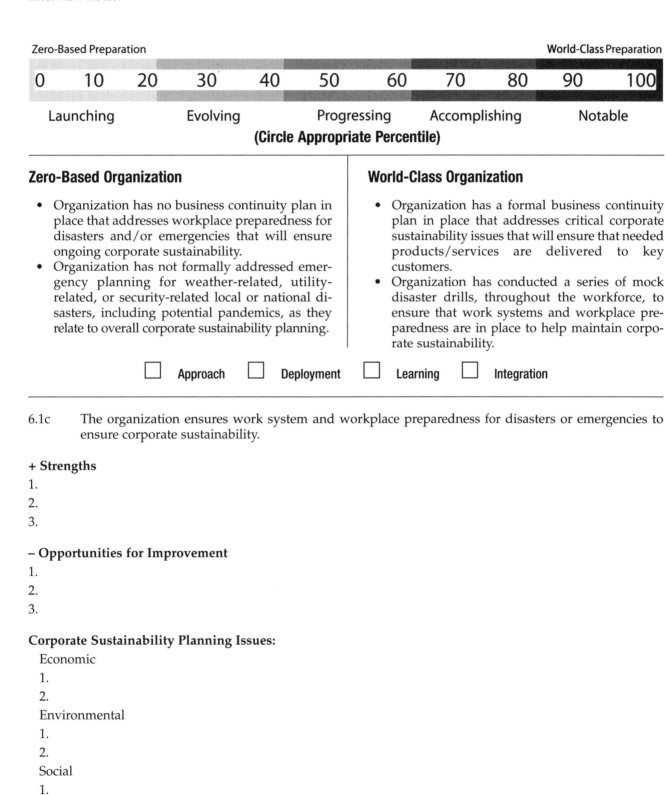

Zero-Based Preparation   World-Class Preparation

| 0 | 10 | 20 | 30 | 40 | 50 | 60 | 70 | 80 | 90 | 100 |

Launching   Evolving   Progressing   Accomplishing   Notable

(Circle Appropriate Percentile)

Zero-Based Organization

- Organization has no business continuity plan in place that addresses workplace preparedness for disasters and/or emergencies that will ensure ongoing corporate sustainability.
- Organization has not formally addressed emergency planning for weather-related, utility-related, or security-related local or national disasters, including potential pandemics, as they relate to overall corporate sustainability planning.

World-Class Organization

- Organization has a formal business continuity plan in place that addresses critical corporate sustainability issues that will ensure that needed products/services are delivered to key customers.
- Organization has conducted a series of mock disaster drills, throughout the workforce, to ensure that work systems and workplace preparedness are in place to help maintain corporate sustainability.

☐ Approach   ☐ Deployment   ☐ Learning   ☐ Integration

6.1c   The organization ensures work system and workplace preparedness for disasters or emergencies to ensure corporate sustainability.

+ Strengths

1.

2.

3.

– Opportunities for Improvement

1.

2.

3.

Corporate Sustainability Planning Issues:

Economic

1.

2.

Environmental

1.

2.

Social

1.

2.

6.2 Work Processes (50 pts.)

Describe how your organization designs, implements, manages, and improves its key work processes to deliver customer value and achieve organizational success and sustainability.

PROCESS

QUESTIONS TO ADDRESS

6.2a   How does your organization design and innovate your work processes to meet all key corporate sustainability requirements?

6.2b(1)   How does your organization implement and manage work processes to ensure that they meet design requirements for corporate sustainability?

6.2b(2)   How does your organization control and minimize the overall costs of inspections, tests, and process or performance audits for corporate sustainability work processes?

6.2c   How does your organization improve work processes to achieve better performance, reduce variability, improve products/services, and keep corporate sustainability processes current with business needs and directions?

6.2 Percent Score

☐ Approach   ☐ Deployment   ☐ Learning   ☐ Integration

6.2a How does your organization design and innovate your work processes to meet all key corporate sustainability requirements?

Interview notes:

Zero-Based Preparation | World-Class Preparation

| 0 | 10 | 20 | 30 | 40 | 50 | 60 | 70 | 80 | 90 | 100 |

Launching   Evolving   Progressing   Accomplishing   Notable

(Circle Appropriate Percentile)

Zero-Based Organization

- Organization is not concerned with whether work processes meet key corporate sustainability process requirements.
- Organization has no process in place to ensure that work processes meet key corporate sustainability requirements.

World-Class Organization

- Organization conducts a formal assessment annually of key corporate sustainability processes to ensure that all design requirements are being met.
- Organization interviews a select number of key stakeholders quarterly to gauge the extent that work processes meet all corporate sustainability requirements.

☐ Approach   ☐ Deployment   ☐ Learning   ☐ Integration

6.2a The organization designs and innovates work processes to meet all key corporate sustainability requirements.

+ Strengths
1.
2.
3.

– Opportunities for Improvement
1.
2.
3.

Corporate Sustainability Planning Issues:

Economic
1.
2.
Environmental
1.
2.
Social
1.
2.

6.2b(1)   How does your organization implement and manage work processes to ensure that they meet design requirements for corporate sustainability?

Interview notes:

Zero-Based Preparation   World-Class Preparation

| 0 | 10 | 20 | 30 | 40 | 50 | 60 | 70 | 80 | 90 | 100 |

Launching   Evolving   Progressing   Accomplishing   Notable

(Circle Appropriate Percentile)

Zero-Based Organization	**World-Class Organization**
• Organization does not have a systematic approach to evaluate and improve key corporate sustainability design processes within the organization. • Organization does not evaluate its key corporate sustainability initiatives to ensure better performance, to reduce variability, and to ensure overall effectiveness in the process design.	• Organization has a structured evaluation process to ensure that all processes designed for corporate sustainability meet design requirements, achieve better performance, and reduce variability. • Organization conducts pilot tests on all key sustainability processes to ensure better performance, to reduce variability, and to improve all key corporate sustainability processes.

☐ Approach   ☐ Deployment   ☐ Learning   ☐ Integration

6.2b(1)   The organization implements and manages work processes to ensure that they meet design requirements for corporate sustainability.

+ Strengths
1.
2.
3.

– Opportunities for Improvement
1.
2.
3.

Corporate Sustainability Planning Issues:
Economic
1.
2.
Environmental
1.
2.
Social
1.
2.

6.2b(2) How does your organization control and minimize the overall costs of inspections, tests, and process or performance audits for corporate sustainability work processes?

Interview notes:

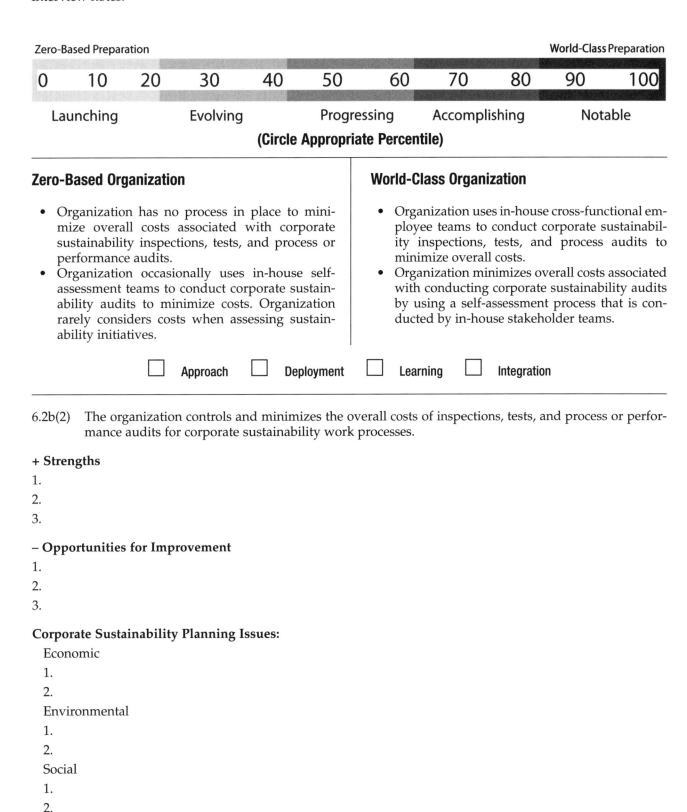

Zero-Based Preparation   World-Class Preparation

| 0 | 10 | 20 | 30 | 40 | 50 | 60 | 70 | 80 | 90 | 100 |

Launching   Evolving   Progressing   Accomplishing   Notable

(Circle Appropriate Percentile)

Zero-Based Organization

- Organization has no process in place to minimize overall costs associated with corporate sustainability inspections, tests, and process or performance audits.
- Organization occasionally uses in-house self-assessment teams to conduct corporate sustainability audits to minimize costs. Organization rarely considers costs when assessing sustainability initiatives.

World-Class Organization

- Organization uses in-house cross-functional employee teams to conduct corporate sustainability inspections, tests, and process audits to minimize overall costs.
- Organization minimizes overall costs associated with conducting corporate sustainability audits by using a self-assessment process that is conducted by in-house stakeholder teams.

☐ Approach   ☐ Deployment   ☐ Learning   ☐ Integration

6.2b(2) The organization controls and minimizes the overall costs of inspections, tests, and process or performance audits for corporate sustainability work processes.

+ Strengths

1.

2.

3.

– Opportunities for Improvement

1.

2.

3.

Corporate Sustainability Planning Issues:

Economic

1.

2.

Environmental

1.

2.

Social

1.

2.

6.2c   How does your organization improve work processes to achieve better performance, reduce variability, improve products/services, and keep corporate sustainability processes current with business needs and directions?

Interview notes:

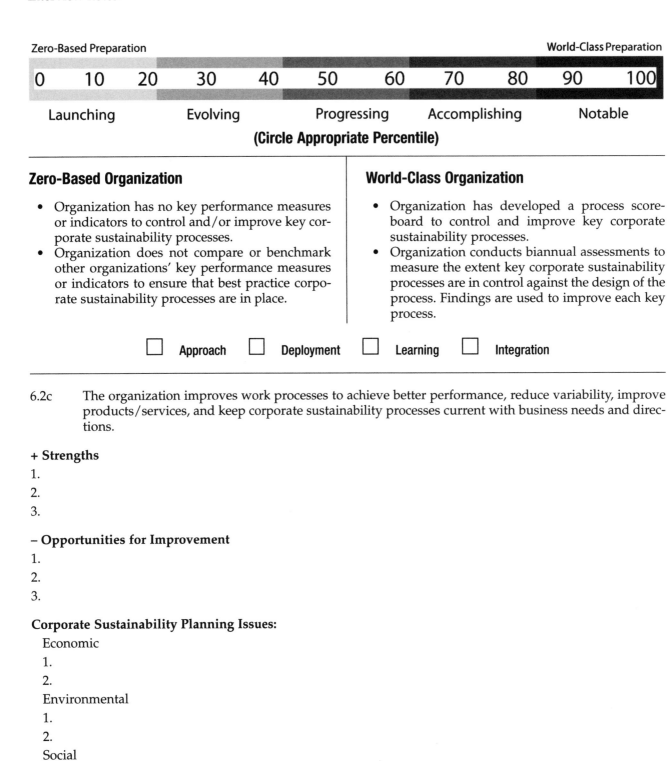

Zero-Based Preparation   World-Class Preparation

| 0 | 10 | 20 | 30 | 40 | 50 | 60 | 70 | 80 | 90 | 100 |

Launching   Evolving   Progressing   Accomplishing   Notable

(Circle Appropriate Percentile)

Zero-Based Organization

- Organization has no key performance measures or indicators to control and/or improve key corporate sustainability processes.
- Organization does not compare or benchmark other organizations' key performance measures or indicators to ensure that best practice corporate sustainability processes are in place.

World-Class Organization

- Organization has developed a process scoreboard to control and improve key corporate sustainability processes.
- Organization conducts biannual assessments to measure the extent key corporate sustainability processes are in control against the design of the process. Findings are used to improve each key process.

☐ Approach   ☐ Deployment   ☐ Learning   ☐ Integration

6.2c   The organization improves work processes to achieve better performance, reduce variability, improve products/services, and keep corporate sustainability processes current with business needs and directions.

+ Strengths
1.
2.
3.

– Opportunities for Improvement
1.
2.
3.

Corporate Sustainability Planning Issues:
Economic
1.
2.
Environmental
1.
2.
Social
1.
2.

NOTES

9 Category 7: Results

7 Results (450 pts.)[17]

The *Results* Category examines how your organization's performance and improvement in all key areas— product outcomes, customer-focused outcomes, financial and market outcomes, workforce-focused outcomes, process effectiveness outcomes, and leadership outcomes ensure corporate sustainability. Performance levels are examined relative to those of competitors and other organizations with similar product offerings that are known for their corporate sustainability results.

Forms can be downloaded from the CD-ROM located inside the back cover of this book.

7.1   Product Outcomes (100 pts.)

Summarize your organization's key product performance results. Segment your results by product offerings, customer groups, and market segments, as appropriate. Include appropriate comparative data.

RESULTS

QUESTIONS TO ADDRESS

7.1a   What are your organization's current levels and trends of product performance that are considered important to customers based on corporate sustainability initiatives?

7.1 Percent Score

☐ Performance Levels   ☐ Trends   ☐ Comparisons   ☐ Linkage   ☐ Gap

7.1a   What are your organization's current levels and trends of product performance that are considered important to customers based on corporate sustainability initiatives?

Interview notes:

Zero-Based Preparation   World-Class Preparation

| 0 | 10 | 20 | 30 | 40 | 50 | 60 | 70 | 80 | 90 | 100 |

Launching   Evolving   Progressing   Accomplishing   Notable

(Circle Appropriate Percentile)

Zero-Based Organization

- Organization collects trend data for customer product/service delivery only during times of high and severe security alerts. Maintenance of corporate sustainability is never a concern.
- Organization does not consistently collect current trend data on product performance based on corporate sustainability and environmental initiatives.

World-Class Organization

- Organization has positive five-year trends for customer product and service performance delivery based on key corporate sustainability initiatives.
- Organization has a three-year positive trend in reducing cycle time for customer product/service checks, based on its corporate sustainability initiatives.

☐ Performance Levels   ☐ Trends   ☐ Comparisons   ☐ Linkage   ☐ Gap

7.1a   The organization's current levels and trends of product performance are considered important to customers based on corporate sustainability initiatives.

+ Strengths
1.
2.
3.

– Opportunities for Improvement
1.
2.
3.

Corporate Sustainability Planning Issues:
Economic
1.
2.
Environmental
1.
2.
Social
1.
2.

7.2   Customer-Focused Outcomes (70 pts.)

Summarize your organization's key product customer-focused results for customer satisfaction, dissatisfaction, and engagement. Segment your results by product offerings, customer groups, and market segments, as appropriate. Include appropriate comparative data.

QUESTIONS TO ADDRESS

7.2a(1)   What are your organization's current levels and trends in customer satisfaction and dissatisfaction with your organization's corporate sustainability initiatives?

7.2a(2)   What are your organization's current levels and trends of customer relationship building and engagement for corporate sustainability initiatives?

7.2 Percent Score

☐ Performance Levels   ☐ Trends   ☐ Comparisons   ☐ Linkage   ☐ Gap

7.2a(1)   What are your organization's current levels and trends in customer satisfaction and dissatisfaction with your organization's corporate sustainability initiatives?

Interview notes:

Zero-Based Preparation   World-Class Preparation

| 0 | 10 | 20 | 30 | 40 | 50 | 60 | 70 | 80 | 90 | 100 |

Launching   Evolving   Progressing   Accomplishing   Notable

(Circle Appropriate Percentile)

Zero-Based Organization

- Organization does not trend customer satisfaction and dissatisfaction data to gauge customer concerns regarding the organization's corporate sustainability initiatives.
- Organization does not collect satisfaction/dissatisfaction data from customers regarding corporate sustainability issues.

World-Class Organization

- Organization collects and trends satisfaction and dissatisfaction data to gauge its customers' ongoing satisfaction with their corporate sustainability initiatives that involve customers and customer groups.
- Organization uses customer satisfaction/dissatisfaction trend data to improve its corporate sustainability initiatives that involve customers.

☐ Performance Levels   ☐ Trends   ☐ Comparisons   ☐ Linkage   ☐ Gap

7.2a(1)   The organization is aware of current levels and trends of customer satisfaction and dissatisfaction with its corporate sustainability initiatives.

+ Strengths
1.
2.
3.

– Opportunities for Improvement
1.
2.
3.

Corporate Sustainability Planning Issues:
Economic
1.
2.
Environmental
1.
2.
Social
1.
2.

7.2a(2)   What are your organization's current levels and trends of customer relationship building and engagement for corporate sustainability initiatives?

Interview notes:

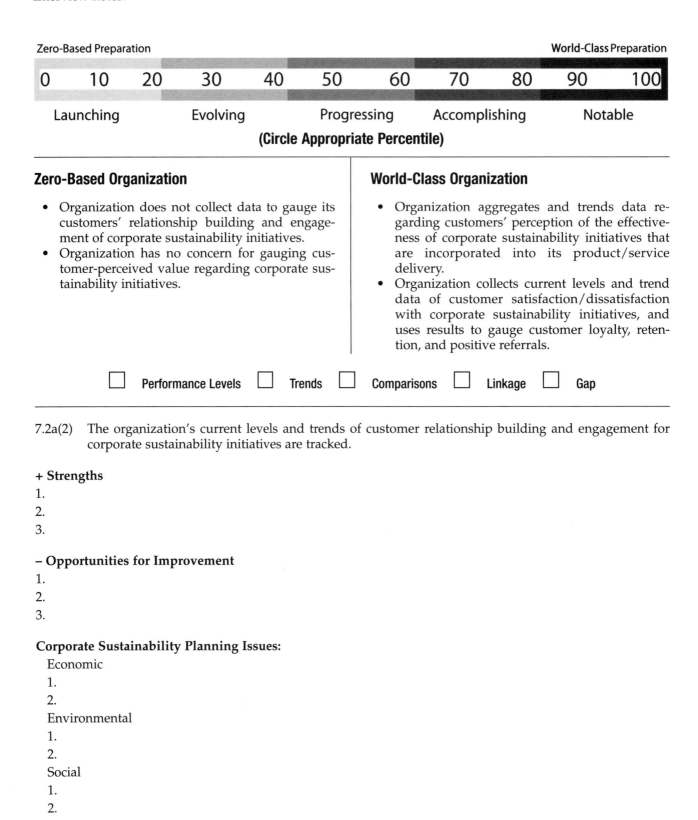

Zero-Based Preparation   World-Class Preparation

| 0 | 10 | 20 | 30 | 40 | 50 | 60 | 70 | 80 | 90 | 100 |

Launching   Evolving   Progressing   Accomplishing   Notable

(Circle Appropriate Percentile)

Zero-Based Organization

- Organization does not collect data to gauge its customers' relationship building and engagement of corporate sustainability initiatives.
- Organization has no concern for gauging customer-perceived value regarding corporate sustainability initiatives.

World-Class Organization

- Organization aggregates and trends data regarding customers' perception of the effectiveness of corporate sustainability initiatives that are incorporated into its product/service delivery.
- Organization collects current levels and trend data of customer satisfaction/dissatisfaction with corporate sustainability initiatives, and uses results to gauge customer loyalty, retention, and positive referrals.

☐ Performance Levels   ☐ Trends   ☐ Comparisons   ☐ Linkage   ☐ Gap

7.2a(2)   The organization's current levels and trends of customer relationship building and engagement for corporate sustainability initiatives are tracked.

+ Strengths
1.
2.
3.

– Opportunities for Improvement
1.
2.
3.

Corporate Sustainability Planning Issues:
Economic
1.
2.
Environmental
1.
2.
Social
1.
2.

7.3 Financial and Market Outcomes (70 pts.)

Summarize your organization's key financial and marketplace performance results by market segments or customer groups, as appropriate. Include appropriate comparative data.

RESULTS

QUESTIONS TO ADDRESS

7.3a(1)   What are your organization's current levels and trends of financial performance that involve corporate sustainability initiatives?

7.3a(2)   What are your organization's current levels and trends of marketplace performance that involve corporate sustainability initiatives?

7.3 Percent Score

☐ Performance Levels   ☐ Trends   ☐ Comparisons   ☐ Linkage   ☐ Gap

7.3a(1)   What are your organization's current levels and trends of financial performance that involve corporate sustainability initiatives?

Interview notes:

Zero-Based Preparation   World-Class Preparation

| 0 | 10 | 20 | 30 | 40 | 50 | 60 | 70 | 80 | 90 | 100 |

Launching   Evolving   Progressing   Accomplishing   Notable

(Circle Appropriate Percentile)

Zero-Based Organization

- Organization has not identified a set of key budgetary and financial measures to gauge overall impact of corporate sustainability initiatives. Many of the measures are inconsistent and anecdotal.
- Organization does not collect trend data on financial performance regarding corporate sustainability.

World-Class Organization

- Organization tracks current levels and trends of financial and market performance to gauge overall effectiveness and impact of corporate sustainability initiatives.
- Organization tracks and trends corporate sustainability expenditures per employee, partner, supplier, and customer. The measures are used to gauge their economic impact against the organization's strategic plans and goals.

☐ Performance Levels   ☐ Trends   ☐ Comparisons   ☐ Linkage   ☐ Gap

7.3a(1)   The organization's current levels and trends of financial performance that involve corporate sustainability initiatives are tracked.

+ Strengths
1.
2.
3.

– Opportunities for Improvement
1.
2.
3.

Corporate Sustainability Planning Issues:
Economic
1.
2.
Environmental
1.
2.
Social
1.
2.

7.3a(2)   What are your organization's current levels and trends of marketplace performance that involve corporate sustainability initiatives?

Interview notes:

Zero-Based Preparation   World-Class Preparation

| 0 | 10 | 20 | 30 | 40 | 50 | 60 | 70 | 80 | 90 | 100 |

| Launching | Evolving | Progressing | Accomplishing | Notable |

(Circle Appropriate Percentile)

Zero-Based Organization

- Organization has not collected data to gauge its marketplace performance involving corporate sustainability initiatives that have been implemented for its key customers over the past three years.
- Organization has not holistically reviewed or collected marketplace performance data that involves its corporate sustainability initiatives.

World-Class Organization

- Organization has a positive three-year trend regarding marketplace performance that involves corporate sustainability initiatives.
- Organization has had positive trends in the market based on its corporate sustainability initiatives with both key customers and suppliers.

☐ Performance Levels   ☐ Trends   ☐ Comparisons   ☐ Linkage   ☐ Gap

7.3a(2)   The organization tracks current levels and trends of marketplace performance that involve corporate sustainability.

+ Strengths
1.
2.
3.

– Opportunities for Improvement
1.
2.
3.

Corporate Sustainability Planning Issues:
Economic
1.
2.
Environmental
1.
2.
Social
1.
2.

7.4 Workforce-Focused Outcomes (70 pts.)

Summarize your organization's key workforce-focused results for workforce engagement and for your workforce environment. Segment your results to address the diversity of your workforce and to address your workforce groups and segments, as appropriate. Include appropriate comparative data.

QUESTIONS TO ADDRESS

7.4a(1)   What are your organization's current levels and trends of workforce engagement and workforce satisfaction that involve corporate sustainability initiatives?

7.4a(2)   What are your organization's current levels and trends of workforce and leader development that involve corporate sustainability initiatives?

7.4a(3)   What are your organization's current levels and trends of workforce capability and capacity, including staffing levels and appropriate skills for corporate sustainability initiatives?

7.4a(4)   What are your organization's current levels and trends of workforce climate, including workforce health, safety, security, and workforce services and benefits that support corporate sustainability?

7.4 Percent Score

☐ Performance Levels   ☐ Trends   ☐ Comparisons   ☐ Linkage   ☐ Gap

7.4a(1) What are your organization's current levels and trends of workforce engagement and workforce satisfaction that involve corporate sustainability initiatives?

Interview notes:

Zero-Based Preparation | World-Class Preparation

| 0 | 10 | 20 | 30 | 40 | 50 | 60 | 70 | 80 | 90 | 100 |

Launching   Evolving   Progressing   Accomplishing   Notable

(Circle Appropriate Percentile)

Zero-Based Organization

- Organization does not measure and trend workforce engagement and satisfaction results that involve corporate sustainability initiatives.
- Organization uses only limited measures to gauge workforce performance that involves corporate sustainability initiatives.

World-Class Organization

- Organization measures and trends data that gauge workforce engagement and satisfaction that are impacted by corporate sustainability initiatives.
- Organization has three-year positive trend results on workforce engagement and satisfaction with key corporate sustainability initiatives.

☐ Performance Levels ☐ Trends ☐ Comparisons ☐ Linkage ☐ Gap

7.4a(1) The organization's current levels and trends of workforce engagement and satisfaction that involve corporate sustainability initiatives are tracked and trended.

+ Strengths

1.

2.

3.

– Opportunities for Improvement

1.

2.

3.

Corporate Sustainability Planning Issues:

Economic

1.

2.

Environmental

1.

2.

Social

1.

2.

7.4a(2)   What are your organization's current levels and trends of workforce and leader development that involve corporate sustainability initiatives?

Interview notes:

Zero-Based Preparation   World-Class Preparation

0	10	20	30	40	50	60	70	80	90	100

| Launching | Evolving | Progressing | Accomplishing | Notable |

(Circle Appropriate Percentile)

Zero-Based Organization

- Organization collects limited data on workforce and leader development that involves corporate sustainability initiatives.
- Organization collects data on workforce and development training that involves corporate sustainability issues, but never uses trend results to gauge progress.

World-Class Organization

- Organization has three-year positive trend results for workforce and leader development that involve corporate sustainability initiatives.
- Organization has experienced a 40 percent increase over three years in the number of employees and leaders who have been trained on corporate sustainability issues.

☐ Performance Levels   ☐ Trends   ☐ Comparisons   ☐ Linkage   ☐ Gap

7.4a(2)   The organization's current levels and trends of workforce and leader development that involve corporate sustainability initiatives are tracked and trended.

+ Strengths

1.

2.

3.

– Opportunities for Improvement

1.

2.

3.

Corporate Sustainability Planning Issues:

Economic

1.

2.

Environmental

1.

2.

Social

1.

2.

7.4a(3)   What are your organization's current levels and trends of workforce capability and capacity, including staffing levels and appropriate skills for corporate sustainability initiatives?

Interview notes:

Zero-Based Preparation   World-Class Preparation

| 0 | 10 | 20 | 30 | 40 | 50 | 60 | 70 | 80 | 90 | 100 |

Launching   Evolving   Progressing   Accomplishing   Notable

(Circle Appropriate Percentile)

Zero-Based Organization

- Organization does not collect trend data on workforce capability and capacity for sustainability initiatives.
- Organization collects no data on workforce staffing levels, certification, and skill levels related to corporate sustainability initiatives.

World-Class Organization

- Organization collects trend data on workforce capability and capacity to ensure that corporate sustainability initiatives are being consistently addressed.
- Organization collects trend data on staffing levels and appropriate employee skills needed to support corporate sustainability efforts.

☐ Performance Levels   ☐ Trends   ☐ Comparisons   ☐ Linkage   ☐ Gap

7.4a(3)   The organization's current levels and trends of workforce capability and capacity, including staffing levels and appropriate skills for corporate sustainability initiatives, are tracked and trended.

+ Strengths

1.
2.
3.

– Opportunities for Improvement

1.
2.
3.

Corporate Sustainability Planning Issues:

Economic

1.
2.

Environmental

1.
2.

Social

1.
2.

7.4a(4)   What are your organization's current levels and trends of workforce climate, including workforce health, safety, security, and workforce services and benefits that support corporate sustainability?

Interview notes:

Zero-Based Preparation   World-Class Preparation

| 0 | 10 | 20 | 30 | 40 | 50 | 60 | 70 | 80 | 90 | 100 |

Launching   Evolving   Progressing   Accomplishing   Notable

(Circle Appropriate Percentile)

Zero-Based Organization

- Organization does not gauge workforce well-being, satisfaction, and dissatisfaction with its corporate sustainability initiatives.
- Organization collects workforce climate data but does not collect data related to workforce health, safety, security, and workforce benefits that support corporate sustainability.

World-Class Organization

- Organization collects and trends data on workforce health, safety, security, and workforce services that support corporate sustainability.
- Organization has collected and trended over three years workforce climate results that involve corporate sustainability issues and initiatives.

☐ Performance Levels   ☐ Trends   ☐ Comparisons   ☐ Linkage   ☐ Gap

7.4a(4)   The organization's current levels and trends of workforce, including workforce health, safety, security, and workforce services and benefits that support corporate sustainability are tracked and trended.

+ Strengths

1.

2.

3.

– Opportunities for Improvement

1.

2.

3.

Corporate Sustainability Planning Issues:

Economic

1.

2.

Environmental

1.

2.

Social

1.

2.

7.5 Process Effectiveness Outcomes (70 pts.)

Summarize your organization's key operational performance results that contribute to the improvement of organizational effectiveness, including your organization's readiness for emergencies. Segment your results by product offerings, by customer groups and market segments, and by processes and locations, as appropriate. Include appropriate comparative data.

QUESTIONS TO ADDRESS

7.5a(1)   What are your organization's current levels and trends of the operational performance of your key work systems and workplace preparedness for disasters or emergencies that support corporate sustainability?

7.5a(2)   What are your organization's current levels and trends in key measures of operational performance of key work processes, including productivity, cycle time, and other process measures for effectiveness, efficiency, and innovation that support corporate sustainability?

7.5 Percent Score

☐ Performance Levels   ☐ Trends   ☐ Comparisons   ☐ Linkage   ☐ Gap

7.5a(1)   What are your organization's current levels and trends of the operational performance of your key work systems and workplace preparedness for disasters or emergencies that support corporate sustainability?

Interview notes:

Zero-Based Preparation   World-Class Preparation

| 0 | 10 | 20 | 30 | 40 | 50 | 60 | 70 | 80 | 90 | 100 |

Launching   Evolving   Progressing   Accomplishing   Notable

(Circle Appropriate Percentile)

Zero-Based Organization

- Organization does not consistently collect key performance results for workplace preparedness that support corporate sustainability.
- Organization's measures for key operational results for emergency preparedness to support corporate sustainability appear limited.

World-Class Organization

- Organization shows positive levels and trends regarding key business continuity measures that support corporate sustainability by using a productivity index known as Service Quality Indicators (SQIs).
- Organization's value-creation processes for corporate sustainability are identified, tracked, and trended to support workplace safety.

☐ Performance Levels   ☐ Trends   ☐ Comparisons   ☐ Linkage   ☐ Gap

7.5a(1)   The organization tracks current levels and trends of the operational performance of key work systems and workplace preparedness for disasters or emergencies that support corporate sustainability.

+ Strengths

1.
2.
3.

– Opportunities for Improvement

1.
2.
3.

Corporate Sustainability Planning Issues:

Economic

1.
2.

Environmental

1.
2.

Social

1.
2.

7.5a(2)　What are your organization's current levels and trends in key measures of operational performance of key work processes including productivity, cycle time, and other process measures for effectiveness, efficiency, and innovation that support corporate sustainability?

Interview notes:

Zero-Based Preparation　　　　　　　　　　　　　　　　　　　　World-Class Preparation

| 0 | 10 | 20 | 30 | 40 | 50 | 60 | 70 | 80 | 90 | 100 |

Launching　　　　　Evolving　　　　　Progressing　　　Accomplishing　　　Notable

(Circle Appropriate Percentile)

Zero-Based Organization

- Organization does not collect trend data on operational performance of key support processes for corporate sustainability.
- Organization's trend data collected for operational performance of key support processes for corporate sustainability has had a negative decrease of 50 percent over three years.

World-Class Organization

- Organization's levels and trends of operational performance of key support processes for corporate sustainability have four-year positive trends.
- Organization's key measures of key support processes for corporate sustainability support the organization's goals and objectives for workplace safety and effectiveness with three-year positive trends.

☐ Performance Levels　☐ Trends　☐ Comparisons　☐ Linkage　☐ Gap

7.5a(2)　The organization's current levels and trends in key measures of operational performance of key work processes, including productivity, cycle-time, and other process measures for effectiveness, efficiency, and innovation that support corporate sustainability are collected.

+ Strengths
1.
2.
3.

– Opportunities for Improvement
1.
2.
3.

Corporate Sustainability Planning Issues:
Economic
1.
2.
Environmental
1.
2.
Social
1.
2.

7.6   Leadership Outcomes (70 pts.)

Summarize your organization's key governance and senior leadership results, including evidence of strategic plan accomplishments, fiscal accountability, legal compliance, ethical behavior, societal responsibility, and support of key communities. Segment your results by organizational units, as appropriate. Include appropriate comparative data.

RESULTS

QUESTIONS TO ADDRESS

7.6a(1)   What are your organization's results for accomplishment of organizational strategy and action plans that involve corporate sustainability initiatives?

7.6a(2)   What are your organization's key current findings and trends in governance and fiscal accountability for corporate sustainability initiatives?

7.6a(3)   What are your organization's results for regulatory and legal compliance that involve corporate sustainability initiatives?

7.6a(4)   What are your organization's key measures of ethical behavior and stakeholder trust in senior leaders and governance related to corporate sustainability initiatives?

7.6a(5)   What are your organization's results for support of its societal responsibilities and key communities' corporate sustainability efforts?

7.6 Percent Score

☐ Performance Levels   ☐ Trends   ☐ Comparisons   ☐ Linkage   ☐ Gap

7.6a(1)   What are your organization's results for accomplishment of organizational strategy and action plans that involve corporate sustainability initiatives?

Interview notes:

Zero-Based Preparation   World-Class Preparation

| 0 | 10 | 20 | 30 | 40 | 50 | 60 | 70 | 80 | 90 | 100 |

Launching   Evolving   Progressing   Accomplishing   Notable

(Circle Appropriate Percentile)

Zero-Based Organization

- Organization does not collect results data for accomplishment of its strategies and action plans for corporate sustainability.
- Organization has no consistent method for collecting data and measuring results for accomplishment of strategies and action plans that involve corporate sustainability initiatives.

World-Class Organization

- Organization has accomplished 92 percent of the strategies and action plans that involve corporate sustainability initiatives.
- Organization collects results data on completion of strategies and action plans that involve corporate sustainability initiatives. The organization has experienced a 98 percent accomplishment rate.

☐ Performance Levels   ☐ Trends   ☐ Comparisons   ☐ Linkage   ☐ Gap

7.6a(1)   The organization tracks results for accomplishment of organizational strategy and action plans that involve corporate sustainability initiatives.

+ Strengths

1.

2.

3.

– Opportunities for Improvement

1.

2.

3.

Corporate Sustainability Planning Issues:

Economic

1.

2.

Environmental

1.

2.

Social

1.

2.

7.6a(2)   What are your organization's key current findings and trends in governance and fiscal accountability for corporate sustainability initiatives?

Interview notes:

Zero-Based Preparation   World-Class Preparation

| 0 | 10 | 20 | 30 | 40 | 50 | 60 | 70 | 80 | 90 | 100 |

Launching   Evolving   Progressing   Accomplishing   Notable

(Circle Appropriate Percentile)

Zero-Based Organization

- Organization does not collect consistent data regarding governance and fiscal accountability for corporate sustainability initiatives.
- Organization collects limited data and trends for governance and fiscal accountability for corporate sustainability initiatives.

World-Class Organization

- Organization's findings and trends for governance and fiscal accountability for corporate sustainability initiatives show a positive three-year trend.
- Organization shows a positive four-year trend regarding governance and fiscal accountability for corporate sustainability initiatives. Data are used to identify additional risk factors and to address auditor recommendations.

☐ Performance Levels   ☐ Trends   ☐ Comparisons   ☐ Linkage   ☐ Gap

7.6a(2)   The organization's key current findings and trends of governance and fiscal accountability for corporate sustainability initiatives are tracked and trended.

+ Strengths
1.
2.
3.

– Opportunities for Improvement
1.
2.
3.

Corporate Sustainability Planning Issues:
Economic
1.
2.
Environmental
1.
2.
Social
1.
2.

7.6a(3)   What are your organization's results for regulatory and legal compliance that involve corporate sustainability initiatives?

Interview notes:

Zero-Based Preparation   World-Class Preparation

| 0 | 10 | 20 | 30 | 40 | 50 | 60 | 70 | 80 | 90 | 100 |

Launching   Evolving   Progressing   Accomplishing   Notable

(Circle Appropriate Percentile)

Zero-Based Organization

- Organization does not consistently collect regulatory and legal compliance data for corporate sustainability issues.
- Organization collects limited regulatory and legal corporate sustainability compliance results outside of what is mandated by state and federal agencies.

World-Class Organization

- Organization collects data and trends results over three years for regulatory and legal compliance issues that involve corporate sustainability issues.
- Organization collects and trends data on corporate sustainability regulatory and legal compliance issues and uses results to improve compliance throughout the organization.

☐ Performance Levels   ☐ Trends   ☐ Comparisons   ☐ Linkage   ☐ Gap

7.6a(3)   The organization's results for regulatory and legal compliance that involve corporate sustainability initiatives are tracked and trended.

+ Strengths

1.

2.

3.

– Opportunities for Improvement

1.

2.

3.

Corporate Sustainability Planning Issues:

Economic

1.

2.

Environmental

1.

2.

Social

1.

2.

7.6a(4)   What are your organization's key measures of ethical behavior and stakeholder trust in senior leaders and governance related to corporate sustainability initiatives?

Interview notes:

Zero-Based Preparation   World-Class Preparation

| 0 | 10 | 20 | 30 | 40 | 50 | 60 | 70 | 80 | 90 | 100 |

Launching   Evolving   Progressing   Accomplishing   Notable

(Circle Appropriate Percentile)

Zero-Based Organization

- Organization does not have measures in place to gauge ethical behavior and stakeholder trust regarding corporate sustainability policies and procedures.
- Organization collects no data on ethical behavior and stakeholder trust regarding corporate sustainability issues and initiatives.

World-Class Organization

- Organization measures senior leaders, employees, customers, partners, and suppliers against a documented ethical code of standards for corporate sustainability.
- Organization ensures that all senior leaders, employees, partners, suppliers, and customers go through a periodic ethics audit regarding adherence to the organization's corporate sustainability policies and procedures.

☐ Performance Levels   ☐ Trends   ☐ Comparisons   ☐ Linkage   ☐ Gap

7.6a(4)   The organization collects key measures of ethical behavior and stakeholder trust in senior leaders and governance related to corporate sustainability initiatives.

+ Strengths
1.
2.
3.

– Opportunities for Improvement
1.
2.
3.

Corporate Sustainability Planning Issues:
Economic
1.
2.
Environmental
1.
2.
Social
1.
2.

7.6a(5)   What are your organization's results for support of its societal responsibilities and key communities' corporate sustainability efforts?

Interview notes:

Zero-Based Preparation   World-Class Preparation

| 0 | 10 | 20 | 30 | 40 | 50 | 60 | 70 | 80 | 90 | 100 |

Launching   Evolving   Progressing   Accomplishing   Notable

(Circle Appropriate Percentile)

Zero-Based Organization

- Organization does not collect and trend corporate sustainability results that support communities in which the organization is located.
- Organization never considers collecting and trending key indicators that support a community's sustainability efforts and initiatives.

World-Class Organization

- Organization collects and trends corporate sustainability results that support communities where the organization is located.
- Organization aligns and compares its corporate sustainability trends and results with societal and community results to support an integrated effort that supports sustainability community-wide.

☐ Performance Levels   ☐ Trends   ☐ Comparisons   ☐ Linkage   ☐ Gap

7.6a(5)   The organization's results for support of its societal responsibilities and key communities corporate sustainability efforts are tracked and trended.

+ Strengths

1.

2.

3.

– Opportunities for Improvement

1.

2.

3.

Corporate Sustainability Planning Issues:

Economic

1.

2.

Environmental

1.

2.

Social

1.

2.

NOTES

Corporate Sustainability Score Sheet

Transfer all assessment item percent scores from the category worksheets.

SUMMARY OF ASSESSMENT ITEMS		Total Points Possible A	Percent Score 0–100% (in 10% units) B	Score (AxB) C
1 Leadership				
1.1 Senior Leadership		70	%	
1.2 Governance and Societal Responsibilities		50	%	_____
	CATEGORY TOTAL	120		
				(Sum C)
2 Strategic Planning				
2.1 Strategy Development		40	%	
2.2 Strategy Deployment		45	%	_____
	CATEGORY TOTAL	85		
				(Sum C)
3 Customer Focus				
3.1 Customer Engagement		40	%	
3.2 Voice of the Customer		45	%	_____
	CATEGORY TOTAL	85		
				(Sum C)
4 Measurement, Analysis, and Knowledge Management				
4.1 Measurement, Analysis, and Improvement of Organizational Performance		45	%	
4.2 Management of Information, Knowledge, and Information Technology		45	%	_____
	CATEGORY TOTAL	90		
				(Sum C)

Continued

Forms can be downloaded from the CD-ROM located inside the back cover of this book.

SUMMARY OF ASSESSMENT ITEMS	Total Points Possible A	Percent Score 0–100% (in 10% units) B	Score (AxB) C
5 Workforce Focus			
5.1 Workforce Engagement	45	%	
5.2 Workforce Environment	40	%	_____
CATEGORY TOTAL	85		
			(Sum C)
6 Process Management			
6.1 Work Systems	35	%	
6.2 Work Processes	50	%	_____
CATEGORY TOTAL	85		
			(Sum C)
7 Results			
7.1 Product Outcomes	100	%	
7.2 Customer-Focused Outcomes	70	%	
7.3 Financial and Market Outcomes	70	%	
7.4 Workforce-Focused Outcomes	70	%	
7.5 Process Effectiveness Outcomes	70	%	
7.6 Leadership Outcomes	70	%	_____
CATEGORY TOTAL	450		
			(Sum C)
TOTAL POINTS	1000		_____

Hierarchy of Corporate Sustainability Assessment Needs

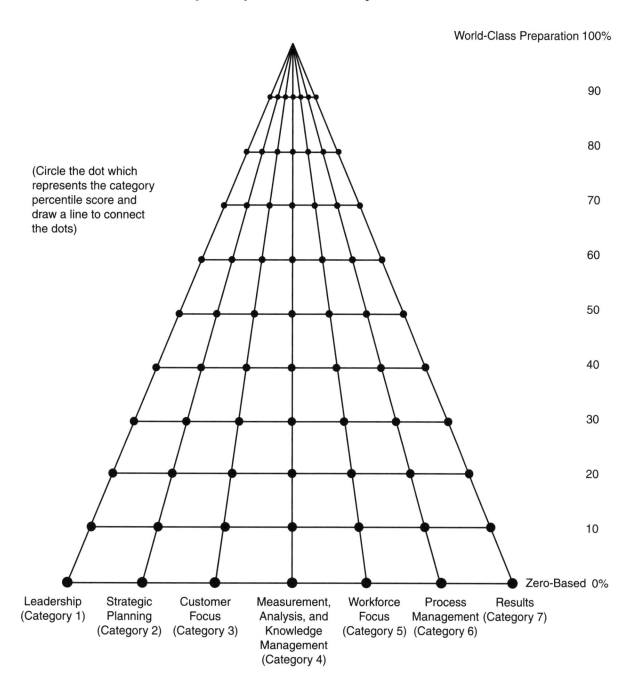

World-Class Preparation 100%

90

80

(Circle the dot which
represents the category
percentile score and
draw a line to connect
the dots)

70

60

50

40

30

20

10

Zero-Based 0%

Leadership (Category 1)

Strategic Planning (Category 2)

Customer Focus (Category 3)

Measurement, Analysis, and Knowledge Management (Category 4)

Workforce Focus (Category 5)

Process Management (Category 6)

Results (Category 7)

Forms can be downloaded from the CD-ROM located inside the back cover of this book.

10 Transforming Assessment Findings into Actionable Strategies for a Corporate Sustainability Plan

The assessment of the organization is complete. Now the next step is to transform the assessment results into actionable short- and long-term strategies for a corporate sustainability plan.

The assessment team should begin this process by reviewing strengths and opportunities for improvement within the areas assessed. The assessment team members will need to reach a consensus on short- and long-term economic, environmental, and social strategic issues for each area. After this process is complete, the team should go back through the assessment manual and collect item percentage scores. The assessment percentages should be shaded within each appropriate item bar graph. Illustrations are given to help the team complete both the assessment bar graphs and strategic planning worksheets.

Forms can be downloaded from the CD-ROM located inside the back cover of this book.

155

Organizational Assessment Bar Graph

(Shade in assessment percentages on bar graphs from item score boxes located throughout workbook.)

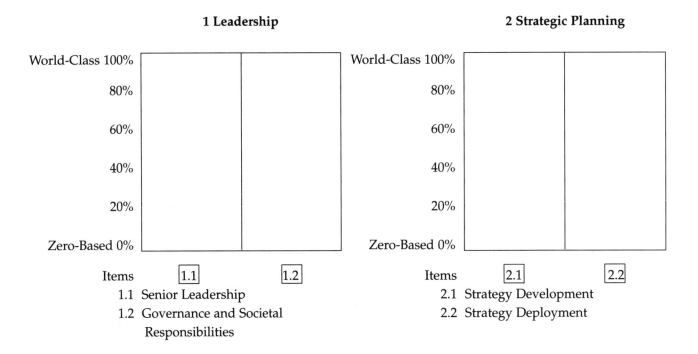

1 Leadership

World-Class 100%
80%
60%
40%
20%
Zero-Based 0%

Items   1.1   1.2

1.1 Senior Leadership
1.2 Governance and Societal
    Responsibilities

2 Strategic Planning

World-Class 100%
80%
60%
40%
20%
Zero-Based 0%

Items   2.1   2.2

2.1 Strategy Development
2.2 Strategy Deployment

Note: Based on bar graphs, select and prioritize within each category short- and long-term economic, environmental, and social strategic issues identified in the assessment and list below.

	1 Leadership Category		**2 Strategic Planning Category**	
Economic	_____ Short-Term	Economic	_____ Short-Term
	_____ Long-Term		_____ Long-Term
Environmental	_____ Short-Term	Environmental	_____ Short-Term
	_____ Long-Term		_____ Long-Term
Social	_____ Short-Term	Social	_____ Short-Term
	_____ Long-Term		_____ Long-Term

Organizational Assessment Bar Graph (Cont.)

(Shade in assessment percentages on bar graphs from item score boxes located throughout workbook.)

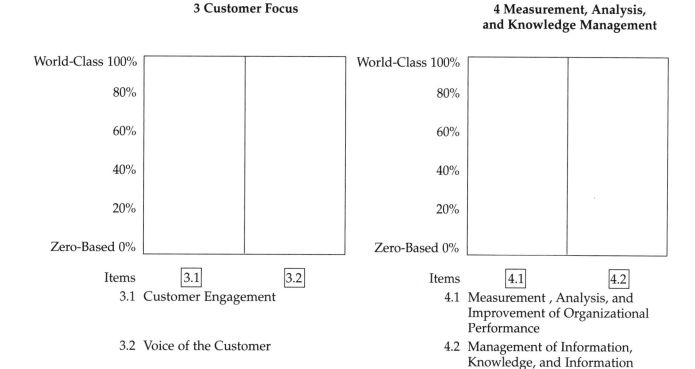

3 Customer Focus

4 Measurement, Analysis, and Knowledge Management

3.1 Customer Engagement

3.2 Voice of the Customer

4.1 Measurement , Analysis, and Improvement of Organizational Performance

4.2 Management of Information, Knowledge, and Information Technology

Note: Based on bar graphs, select and prioritize within each category short- and long-term economic, environmental, and social strategic issues identified in the assessment and list below.

3 Customer Focus Category		
Economic	_____	Short-Term
	_____	Long-Term
Environmental	_____	Short-Term
	_____	Long-Term
Social	_____	Short-Term
	_____	Long-Term

4 Measurement, Analysis, and Knowledge Management Category		
Economic	_____	Short-Term
	_____	Long-Term
Environmental	_____	Short-Term
	_____	Long-Term
Social	_____	Short-Term
	_____	Long-Term

Organizational Assessment Bar Graph (Cont.)

(Shade in assessment percentages on bar graphs from item score boxes located throughout workbook.)

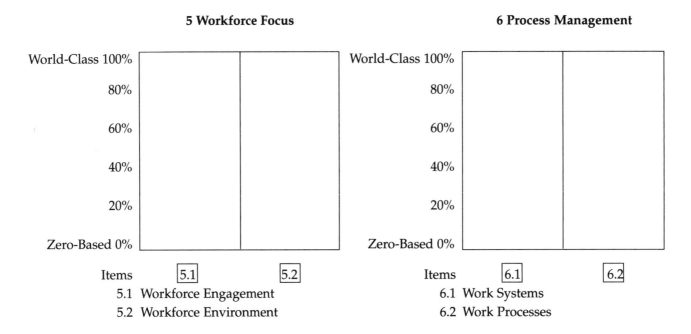

5 Workforce Focus

World-Class 100%
80%
60%
40%
20%
Zero-Based 0%

Items   5.1   5.2

5.1 Workforce Engagement
5.2 Workforce Environment

6 Process Management

World-Class 100%
80%
60%
40%
20%
Zero-Based 0%

Items   6.1   6.2

6.1 Work Systems
6.2 Work Processes

Note: Based on bar graphs, select and prioritize within each category short- and long-term economic, environmental, and social strategic issues identified in the assessment and list below.

	5 Workforce Focus **Category**			**6 Process Management** **Category**	
Economic	_____	Short-Term	Economic	_____	Short-Term
	_____	Long-Term		_____	Long-Term
Environmental	_____	Short-Term	Environmental	_____	Short-Term
	_____	Long-Term		_____	Long-Term
Social	_____	Short-Term	Social	_____	Short-Term
	_____	Long-Term		_____	Long-Term

Organizational Assessment Bar Graph (Cont.)

(Shade in assessment percentages on bar graphs from item score boxes located throughout workbook.)

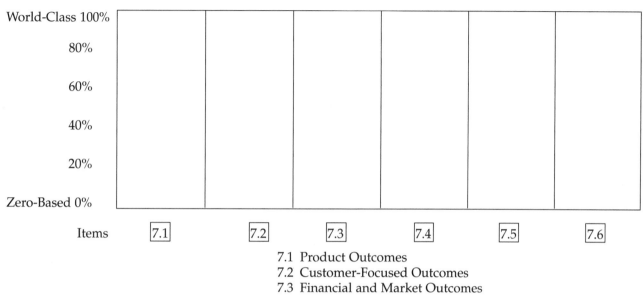

7 Results

7.1 Product Outcomes
7.2 Customer-Focused Outcomes
7.3 Financial and Market Outcomes
7.4 Workforce-Focused Outcomes
7.5 Process Effectiveness Outcomes
7.6 Leadership Outcomes

Note: Based on bar graphs, select and prioritize within each category short- and long-term economic, environmental, and social issues identified in the assessment and list below.

7 Results
Category

Economic _____ Short-Term

_____ Long-Term

Environmental _____ Short-Term

_____ Long-Term

Social _____ Short-Term

_____ Long-Term

The shaded bar graphs will help the assessment team identify specific items within each category of the organization that need improvement as corporate sustainability issues.

The next step for the team after all scores have been shaded in on the bar graphs is to select and prioritize short- and long-term strategic planning issues within each category that were previously identified through the assessment process by the team. The team will go through the process of prioritizing the strategic short- and long-term economic, environmental, and social planning issues within each category that need to be developed into actionable improvement strategies for the organization (see Illustration 1).

A master strategic planning worksheet for corporate sustainability is included on the accompanying CD-ROM for the teams to use to list their prioritized short- and long-term initiatives. The appropriate category, term, and priority should be circled, detailing the specific initiative. Action item(s) should be listed in respective order to accomplish the identified strategies. In addition, individual responsibilities and review and completion dates should be documented to transform the organization's strategic initiatives into actionable improvement. Illustration 2 details how to complete a strategic planning worksheet for corporate sustainability planning.

The strategic planning worksheet for corporate sustainability should be completed by the assessment team (see Illustration 2). The results of both the assessment and the identified strategic issues for corporate sustainability should be reported back to the organization's senior leadership and ultimately integrated into the organization's annual short- and long-term strategic planning process. See corporate sustainability plan and budget forms on the accompanying CD-ROM to develop a complete corporate sustainability plan based on assessment findings.

ILLUSTRATION 1

1 Leadership

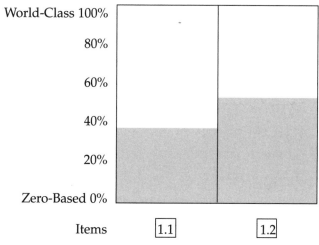

Items   1.1   1.2

1.1 Senior Leadership
1.2 Governance and Societal Responsibilities

Note: Based on bar graphs, select and prioritize within each category short- and long-term economic, environmental, and social strategic issues identified in the assessment and list below.

Economic   Senior leadership to develop a corporate sustainability plan _____ Short-Term

Senior leadership to assess organization for corporate sustainability issues and vulnerabilities as they relate to economic vitality for the organization. _____ Long-Term

Environmental   Align organization's corporate sustainability plan with the corporate environmental plan _____ Short-Term

President and staff to develop corporate sustainability video for organization that promotes environmental issues. _____ Long-Term

Social   Develop vision and mission statements for the organization. _____ Short-Term

Senior management to develop a formal employee recognition system for corporate sustainability that promotes social responsibility. _____ Long-Term

ILLUSTRATION 2
STRATEGIC PLANNING WORKSHEEET FOR A CORPORATE SUSTAINABILITY PLAN

Category (circle one)

1 Leadership

2 Strategic Planning

3 Customer Focus

4 Measurement, Analysis, and Knowledge Management

5 Workforce Focus

6 Process Management

7 Results

Term (circle one)

Short term: one to two years

Long term: more than two years

Priority (circle one)   Economic   Environmental   Social   <u>Senior leadership to develop a corporate sustainability plan</u>

ACTION ITEMS (Steps to accomplish strategy)	WHO IS RESPONSIBLE	REVIEW DATE	COMPLETION DATE
1. Define corporate sustainability issues and vulnerabilities.	President	January 10	February 28
2. Form a senior management team to review corporate sustainability issues.	Vice President	February 5	March 15
3. Cross-functional employee team to develop plan.	Director	March 30	April 10
4. Senior staff finalizes corporate sustainability plan.	President and Vice Presidents	April 15	May 15
5. Distribute plan to employees, suppliers, customers, and partners.	Managers	May 29	June 29
6.			
7.			
8.			
9.			
10.			

List action items in respective order   List individual responsibilities by names or position   List review dates   List completion dates

STRATEGIC PLANNING WORKSHEEET FOR A CORPORATE SUSTAINABILITY PLAN

Category (circle one)

1 Leadership

2 Strategic Planning

3 Customer Focus

4 Measurement, Analysis, and Knowledge Management

5 Workforce Focus

6 Process Management

7 Results

Priority (circle one)   Economic   Environmental   Social   _____

Term (circle one)

Short term: one to two years

Long term: more than two years

ACTION ITEMS (Steps to accomplish strategy)	WHO IS RESPONSIBLE	REVIEW DATE	COMPLETION DATE
1.			
2.			
3.			
4.			
5.			
6.			
7.			
8.			
9.			
10			

Forms can be downloaded from the CD-ROM located inside the back cover of this book.

A Quick and Easy Supplier/Customer Assessment for Corporate Sustainability

Reasons for Conducting a Corporate Sustainability Assessment for Suppliers and Customers

- To align your organization's sustainability initiatives with its suppliers/customers to save and reduce costs
- To receive a *results-oriented* supplier/customer review of sustainability efforts
- To gain a knowledge of the various supplier/customer sustainability initiatives
- To identify supplier/customer strengths and opportunities for sustainability improvements
- To improve overall supplier/customer performance regarding corporate sustainability
- To use as a tool to gauge supplier/customer progress in meeting sustainability compliance issues
- To use assessment results to help suppliers/customers develop a corporate sustainability plan
- To encourage suppliers/customers to view sustainability planning as a competitive issue

The Corporate Sustainability Assessment ensures that your organization's suppliers and customers are focused on sustainability issues and aligning their sustainability goals with those of your organization.

Forms can be downloaded from the CD-ROM located inside the back cover of this book.

Organizational Profile for Corporate Sustainability

Name: _____   Date: _____

Check One:

□ Supplier   □ Customer   □ Other

Organizational Environment (Describe how the organization's main products, offerings, and services are impacted by sustainability issues.)

Organizational Relationship (Describe how the organization meets sustainability needs of key customer segments, stakeholder groups, suppliers, and partners.)

Competitive Environment (Describe organization's competitive position and approach to addressing sustainability issues relative to other comparable organizations delivering similar products, offerings, and services.)

Strategic Challenges (Describe how the organization's key operations, human resources, and community-related challenges are impacted by sustainability issues.)

Performance Improvement System (Describe the organization's overall approach to performance improvement and systematic evaluation of its sustainability initiatives.)

Supplier/Customer Corporate Sustainability Assessment Evaluation Dimensions

The organization scoring system is based on three evaluation dimensions: (1) approach, (2) deployment, and (3) results. All three dimensions should be considered before assigning a score.

The Three Assessment Dimensions

Approach

Approach refers to the method(s) the organization uses to accomplish its sustainability activity. The scoring criteria used to evaluate the approach may include one or more of the following, as appropriate:

- The effectiveness of the use of methods, tools, and techniques
- The degree to which the approach embodies effective evaluation/improvement cycles
- The degree to which the approach is based upon quantitative information that is objective and reliable
- The degree to which the approach is prevention-based
- The uniqueness and innovativeness of the approach, including significant and effective new adaptations of tools and techniques used in other corporate applications
- The uniqueness of the approach

Deployment

Deployment refers to the extent to which the organization applies and/or distributes its sustainability activity among employees, customers, suppliers, stakeholders, and/or departments. The scoring criteria used to evaluate deployment may include one or more of the following, as appropriate:

- The appropriate and effective application among employees, customers, suppliers, stakeholders, and/or departments
- The appropriate and effective application to all transactions and interactions with employees, customers, suppliers, stakeholders, and/or departments
- The activity involves all employees
- The activity is applied in all departments

Results

Results refers to outcomes the organization achieves when applying its sustainability activity. The scoring criteria used to evaluate results may include one or more of the following, as appropriate:

- The rate of quality and performance improvement
- The breadth of quality and performance improvement
- The demonstration of sustained performance improvement
- The comparison with competitive and/or *best practice* organization initiatives
- The organization's ability to show that improvement results were derived from its strategic initiatives

Guidelines for the Supplier/Customer Corporate Sustainability Assessment

Introduction

The assessment is a carefully considered evaluation resulting in an opinion or judgment of the effectiveness and efficiency of the organization and the maturity of the organization's corporate sustainability performance management system. Self-Assessment is usually performed by the organization's own employees. The intent of the assessment is to provide fact-based guidance to the organization regarding where to invest resources for sustainability improvement.

The assessment is intended to provide an approach to determine the relative degree of maturity of the organization's corporate sustainability performance management systems and to identify the main areas of sustainability improvement. Specific features of the organizational self-assessment approach for corporate sustainability are that it can:

- Be applied to the entire organizational performance management system
- Be completed quickly with internal resources
- Be completed by a multi-discipline team, or by one person in the organization who is supported by senior leadership
- Identify and facilitate the prioritization of the organization's strengths and opportunities for improvement
- Facilitate maturing and aligning of the organization's sustainability initiatives and developing a corporate sustainability plan

Supplier/Customer Self-Assessment Scoring Profile

Approach/Deployment		
Maturity Level	**Performance Level**	**Guidance**
0	Approach	No Approach/Anecdotal
1 (Launching)	Approach	Good Approach/No Deployment
2 (Evolving)	Approach	Systematic Approach/Not Fully Deployed
3 (Progressing)	Deployment	Sound Approach/Partial Deployment
4 (Accomplishing)	Deployment	Sound Approach/Mostly Deployed
5 (Notable)	Deployment	Sound Approach/Full Deployment

Results		
Maturity Level	**Performance Level**	**Guidance**
0	Results	No Performance Results/Anecdotal
1 (Launching)	Results	Some Performance Results
2 (Evolving)	Results	Good Performance Results
3 (Progressing)	Results	Some Trends/Good Results
4 (Accomplishing)	Results	Many Improvement Trends/Good Results
5 (Notable)	Results	Excellent Trends/Sustained Results

Assessment Improvement Plan

List strengths and opportunities based on assessment. Align and transform key findings into a corporate sustainability plan.

Strengths

Opportunities

Sustainability Planning Issues
    Economic Dimension
    1.

    2.

    Environmental Dimension
    1.

    2.

    Social Dimension
    1.

    2.

1 Leadership

(Circle one)

1. Senior Leadership sets and deploys the organization's values, strategic directions, and performance expectations of sustainability initiatives.

0	1	2	3	4	5
Approach			Deployment		

2. Senior Leaders create an environment for empowerment, innovation, safety, and equity for all employees regarding sustainability issues.

0	1	2	3	4	5
Approach			Deployment		

3. Organization's corporate sustainability governance issues are addressed by senior leadership (that is, management accountability for the organization's action, fiscal accountability, independent internal/external audits, and protection of stakeholder interests.)

0	1	2	3	4	5
Approach			Deployment		

4. Senior leaders review the organization's sustainability performance and capabilities relative to competitors and comparable organizations short/longer term goals, and achievements.

0	1	2	3	4	5
Approach			Deployment		

5. Senior leaders identify, review, and share with stakeholders key performance measures for corporate sustainability initiatives on a regular basis.

0	1	2	3	4	5
Approach			Deployment		

6. Senior leaders translate key performance review findings for corporate sustainability into priorities for organization improvements.

0	1	2	3	4	5
Approach			Deployment		

7. Organization leaders' performance regarding sustainability issues is reviewed by key stakeholders and the findings are used to improve their leadership effectiveness.

0	1	2	3	4	5
Approach			Deployment		

8. The organization anticipates and addresses the impact that its sustainability programs, offerings, services, and operations have on the communities it serves both currently and in the future.

0	1	2	3	4	5
Approach			Deployment		

9. The organization ensures ethical behavior in all transactions and interactions involving corporate sustainability initiatives.

0	1	2	3	4	5
Approach			Deployment		

10. The organization actively supports and strengthens corporate sustainability initiatives within communities in which it is located.

0	1	2	3	4	5
Approach			Deployment		

✔ **Documentation**

☐ _____
☐ _____
☐ _____
☐ _____
☐ _____
☐ _____
☐ _____
☐ _____
☐ _____
☐ _____
☐ _____
☐ _____
☐ _____
☐ _____
☐ _____
☐ _____
☐ _____
☐ _____
☐ _____

To score, add the circled numbers together and divide by 10. Transfer score to (Supplement 1) Radar Graph.

Average Score ☐

Note: List documents that support assessment findings.

Assessment Improvement Plan

List strengths and opportunities based on assessment. Align and transform key findings into a corporate sustainability plan.

Strengths

Opportunities

Sustainability Planning Issues
    Economic Dimension
    1.

    2.

    Environmental Dimension
    1.

    2

    .

    Social Dimension
    1.

    2.

2 Strategic Planning

(Circle one)

1. The organization's overall corporate sustainability strategic planning process involves all key stakeholders.

0	1	2	3	4	5
Approach			Deployment		

2. The organization's strategic planning for corporate sustainability addresses environment, programs, offerings, technology, resources, budgetary, ethical responsibilities, supplier/customer needs, and regulatory issues.

0	1	2	3	4	5
Approach			Deployment		

3. The organization has documented its strategic objectives for corporate sustainability and has published a timetable for accomplishing them.

0	1	2	3	4	5
Approach			Deployment		

4. The organization's strategic objectives for corporate sustainability balance the needs of employees and key stakeholders.

0	1	2	3	4	5
Approach			Deployment		

5. The organization has developed and deployed action plans to employees to achieve its key strategic objectives for corporate sustainability.

0	1	2	3	4	5
Approach			Deployment		

6. The organization has identified and shared with all key stakeholders its short- and longer-term action plans for corporate sustainability.

0	1	2	3	4	5
Approach			Deployment		

7. The organization has identified human resource plans within its strategic objectives and has published action plans to ensure progress toward meeting its goals for corporate sustainability.

0	1	2	3	4	5
Approach			Deployment		

8. The organization has identified key performance indicators for tracking action plan progress of its corporate sustainability plan.

0	1	2	3	4	5
Approach			Deployment		

9. The organization has identified performance projections with time horizons for its strategic objectives for corporate sustainability.

0	1	2	3	4	5
Approach			Deployment		

10. The organization has based its short- and longer-term performance projections on competitors, comparable organizations, benchmarks, goals, and/or past corporate sustainability performance.

0	1	2	3	4	5
Approach			Deployment		

To score, add the circled numbers together and divide by 10. Transfer score to (Supplement 1) Radar Graph.

Average Score

✔ Documentation

☐ _____
☐ _____
☐ _____
☐ _____
☐ _____
☐ _____
☐ _____
☐ _____
☐ _____
☐ _____
☐ _____
☐ _____
☐ _____
☐ _____
☐ _____
☐ _____
☐ _____
☐ _____
☐ _____

Note: List documents that support assessment findings.

Assessment Improvement Plan

List strengths and opportunities based on assessment. Align and transform key findings into a corporate sustainability plan.

Strengths

Opportunities

Sustainability Planning Issues
   Economic Dimension
   1.

   2.

   Environmental Dimension
   1.

   2.

   Social Dimension
   1.

   2.

3 Customer Focus

(Circle one)

1. The organization has a method to determine and target customer segments and markets that its corporate sustainability program will address.

0	1	2	3	4	5
Approach			Deployment		

2. The organization has methods to listen and learn from current, former, and future customers and stakeholders regarding requirements and expectations of corporate sustainability offerings and services.

0	1	2	3	4	5
Approach			Deployment		

3. The organization keeps its listening and learning methods current with corporate sustainability service needs and directions (that is, focus groups, surveys, and various other listening and learning methods.)

0	1	2	3	4	5
Approach			Deployment		

4. The organization builds relationships by providing corporate sustainability initiatives to increase loyalty, satisfy, and retain customers.

0	1	2	3	4	5
Approach			Deployment		

5. The organization ensures that a consistent corporate sustainability approach is in place for employees who have direct contact with customers/stakeholders.

0	1	2	3	4	5
Approach			Deployment		

6. The organization ensures that its customer relationship skills are kept current with corporate sustainability service needs and directions.

0	1	2	3	4	5
Approach			Deployment		

7. The organization has a method to determine customer satisfaction and dissatisfaction with corporate sustainability initiatives.

0	1	2	3	4	5
Approach			Deployment		

8. The organization has a consistent customer follow-up procedure for its corporate sustainability initiative programs, services, and offerings that ensures prompt and actionable feedback.

0	1	2	3	4	5
Approach			Deployment		

9. The organization compares its customer satisfaction with corporate sustainability initiatives against competitive and/or comparable organizations that deliver similar services.

0	1	2	3	4	5
Approach			Deployment		

10. The organization keeps its methods for determining customer satisfaction with corporate sustainability initiatives current with service needs and directions (that is, focus groups, surveys, and various other customer satisfaction methods.).

0	1	2	3	4	5
Approach			Deployment		

To score, add the circled numbers together and divide by 10. Transfer score to (Supplement 1) Radar Graph.

Average Score [ ]

✔ Documentation

☐ _____
☐ _____
☐ _____
☐ _____
☐ _____
☐ _____
☐ _____
☐ _____
☐ _____
☐ _____
☐ _____
☐ _____
☐ _____
☐ _____
☐ _____
☐ _____
☐ _____
☐ _____
☐ _____

Note: List documents that support assessment findings.

Assessment Improvement Plan

List strengths and opportunities based on assessment. Align and transform key findings into a corporate sustainability plan.

Strengths

Opportunities

Sustainability Planning Issues
    Economic Dimension
    1.

    2.

    Environmental Dimension
    1.

    2.

    Social Dimension
    1.

    2.

4 Measurement, Analysis, and Knowledge Management

(Circle one)

1. The organization selects, collects, aligns, and integrates corporate sustainability data and information for tracking daily operations and overall organization performance.

0	1	2	3	4	5
Approach			Deployment		

2. The organization has a selection process for corporate sustainability initiatives to collect key comparative data and information to support operational, strategic decision making, and innovation.

0	1	2	3	4	5
Approach			Deployment		

3. The organization keeps its performance measurement system for corporate sustainability current with organization needs and directions.

0	1	2	3	4	5
Approach			Deployment		

4. The organization collects data and information that support senior leadership's direction to accomplish the organization's corporate sustainability strategic plans.

0	1	2	3	4	5
Approach			Deployment		

5. The organization's leadership communicates to employees corporate sustainability data and information results that support its decision making.

0	1	2	3	4	5
Approach			Deployment		

6. The organization makes needed corporate sustainability data and information accessible to employees, stakeholders, and suppliers/customers.

0	1	2	3	4	5
Approach			Deployment		

7. The organization ensures that corporate sustainability hardware and software are reliable, secure, and user-friendly.

0	1	2	3	4	5
Approach			Deployment		

8. The organization keeps corporate sustainability data and information mechanisms, including hardware and software systems, current with its needs and directions.

0	1	2	3	4	5
Approach			Deployment		

9. The organization manages the collection and transfer of corporate sustainability knowledge among employees, stakeholders, and suppliers/customers.

0	1	2	3	4	5
Approach			Deployment		

10. The organization ensures that its data information and organizational knowledge for corporate sustainability are timely, reliable, secure, accurate, confidential, and have integrity.

0	1	2	3	4	5
Approach			Deployment		

✔ Documentation

☐ _____
☐ _____
☐ _____
☐ _____
☐ _____
☐ _____
☐ _____
☐ _____
☐ _____
☐ _____
☐ _____
☐ _____
☐ _____
☐ _____
☐ _____
☐ _____
☐ _____
☐ _____

To score, add the circled numbers together and divide by 10. Transfer score to (Supplement 1) Radar Graph.

Average Score

Note: List documents that support assessment findings.

Assessment Improvement Plan

List strengths and opportunities based on assessment. Align and transform key findings into a corporate sustainability plan.

Strengths

Opportunities

Sustainability Planning Issues
     Economic Dimension
     1.

     2.

     Environmental Dimension
     1.

     2.

     Social Dimension
     1.

     2.

5 Workforce Focus

(Circle one)

1. The organization organizes and manages corporate sustainability initiatives that promote cooperation, initiative, empowerment, and innovation that ensure effective communication and skill sharing among employees.

0	1	2	3	4	5
Approach			Deployment		

2. The organization's corporate sustainability performance management system supports and recognizes high-performance work among employees.

0	1	2	3	4	5
Approach			Deployment		

3. The organization's corporate sustainability initiatives identify characteristics and skills that support its recruiting, hiring, retaining, and career progression of employees.

0	1	2	3	4	5
Approach			Deployment		

4. The organization's employee education and training for corporate sustainability contribute to achievement of action plans and directions.

0	1	2	3	4	5
Approach			Deployment		

5. The organization ensures that education/training given to its employees supports corporate sustainability initiatives.

0	1	2	3	4	5
Approach			Deployment		

6. The organization motivates employees to use their full potential in promoting corporate sustainability issues and initiatives.

0	1	2	3	4	5
Approach			Deployment		

7. The organization reviews and improves workplace health, safety, security, and ergonomics for corporate sustainability.

0	1	2	3	4	5
Approach			Deployment		

8. The organization ensures employee preparedness for corporate sustainability issues.

0	1	2	3	4	5
Approach			Deployment		

9. The organization has an assessment process to determine employee well-being, satisfaction, and motivation regarding corporate sustainability issues.

0	1	2	3	4	5
Approach			Deployment		

10. The organization uses assessment findings to identify and gauge employee corporate sustainability environmental issues.

0	1	2	3	4	5
Approach			Deployment		

✔ **Documentation**

☐ _____
☐ _____
☐ _____
☐ _____
☐ _____
☐ _____
☐ _____
☐ _____
☐ _____
☐ _____
☐ _____
☐ _____
☐ _____
☐ _____
☐ _____
☐ _____
☐ _____
☐ _____

To score, add the circled numbers together and divide by 10. Transfer score to (Supplement 1) Radar Graph.

Average Score

Note: List documents that support assessment findings.

Assessment Improvement Plan

List strengths and opportunities based on assessment. Align and transform key findings into a corporate sustainability plan.

Strengths

Opportunities

Sustainability Planning Issues
    Economic Dimension
    1.

    2.

    Environmental Dimension
    1.

    2.

    Social Dimension
    1.

    2.

6 Process Management

(Circle one)

1. The organization determines value-creation corporate sustainability processes that address market needs and directions for employees and stakeholders (that is, technology skills, problem-solving skills, team involvement, and various other methods.)

0	1	2	3	4	5
Approach			Deployment		

2. The organization determines value-creation corporate sustainability process requirements by incorporating input from employees, stakeholders, and partners.

0	1	2	3	4	5
Approach			Deployment		

3. The organization incorporates new technology and organizational knowledge into the design of value-creation corporate sustainability processes.

0	1	2	3	4	5
Approach			Deployment		

4. The organization has key performance measures for corporate sustainability to control and improve its value-creation processes.

0	1	2	3	4	5
Approach			Deployment		

5. The organization reviews its value-creation corporate sustainability processes to maximize success and improve sustainability programs, offerings, and services.

0	1	2	3	4	5
Approach			Deployment		

6. The organization determines key support processes that support its corporate sustainability offerings (that is, facilities management, secretarial, food service, and various other methods.)

0	1	2	3	4	5
Approach			Deployment		

7. The organization determines key support process requirements for corporate sustainability initiatives by incorporating input from employees, stakeholders, and partners.

0	1	2	3	4	5
Approach			Deployment		

8. The organization incorporates new technology and organizational knowledge into the design of support processes for corporate sustainability.

0	1	2	3	4	5
Approach			Deployment		

9. The organization has in place key performance measures to control and improve support processes of corporate sustainability.

0	1	2	3	4	5
Approach			Deployment		

10. The organization reviews its support processes to achieve better performance, to reduce variability, and to keep them current with its corporate sustainability needs and directions.

0	1	2	3	4	5
Approach			Deployment		

To score, add the circled numbers together and divide by 10. Transfer score to (Supplement 1) Radar Graph.

Average Score

✔ **Documentation**

☐ _____
☐ _____
☐ _____
☐ _____
☐ _____
☐ _____
☐ _____
☐ _____
☐ _____
☐ _____
☐ _____
☐ _____
☐ _____
☐ _____
☐ _____
☐ _____
☐ _____
☐ _____
☐ _____

Note: List documents that support assessment findings.

Assessment Improvement Plan

List strengths and opportunities based on assessment. Align and transform key findings into a corporate sustainability plan.

Strengths

Opportunities

Sustainability Planning Issues
    Economic Dimension
    1.

    2.

    Environmental Dimension
    1.

    2.

    Social Dimension
    1.

    2.

7 Results

(Circle one)

1. The organization collects and trends key supplier/customer results of corporate sustainability initiatives.

0	1	2	3	4	5
Results					

2. The organization collects and trends supplier/customer and stakeholder satisfaction/dissatisfaction corporate sustainability data and compares its results against competitive or comparable organizations.

0	1	2	3	4	5
Results					

3. The organization collects and trends budgetary and financial performance results of corporate sustainability initiatives.

0	1	2	3	4	5
Results					

4. The organization collects and trends performance results of corporate sustainability initiatives.

0	1	2	3	4	5
Results					

5. The organization collects and trends corporate sustainability performance and effectiveness results (that is, employee teamwork, knowledge, and skill-sharing results, and various other results and trends.)

0	1	2	3	4	5
Results					

6. The organization collects and trends employee well-being, satisfaction, and dissatisfaction results for corporate sustainability initiatives.

0	1	2	3	4	5
Results					

7. The organization collects and trends operational performance of key corporate sustainability initiatives.

0	1	2	3	4	5
Results					

8. The organization collects and trends operational performance of key support service results for corporate sustainability (that is, productivity, cycle time, supplier/customer performance, and various other results and trends.)

0	1	2	3	4	5
Results					

9. The organization collects and trends data for fiscal accountability, ethical behavior, and legal compliance of corporate sustainability issues.

0	1	2	3	4	5
Results					

10. The organization collects and trends results data for its community involvement with corporate sustainability initiatives.

0	1	2	3	4	5
Results					

✔ **Documentation**

☐ _____
☐ _____
☐ _____
☐ _____
☐ _____
☐ _____
☐ _____
☐ _____
☐ _____
☐ _____
☐ _____
☐ _____
☐ _____
☐ _____
☐ _____
☐ _____
☐ _____
☐ _____

To score, add the circled numbers together and divide by 10. Transfer score to (Supplement 1) Radar Graph.

Average Score

Note: List documents that support assessment findings.

Supplement 1 - Radar Graph

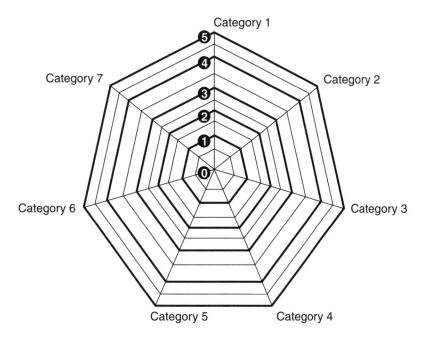

Category 1   Leadership
Category 2   Strategic Planning
Category 3   Customer Focus
Category 4   Measurement, Analysis, and Knowledge Management
Category 5   Workforce Focus
Category 6   Process Management
Category 7   Results

Note: Record average scores from the assessment onto the above radar graph.

Scoring Profile

Zero-Based Preparation   World-Class Preparation

| 0 | 10 | 20 | 30 | 40 | 50 | 60 | 70 | 80 | 90 | 100 |

Launching	Evolving	Progressing	Accomplishing	Notable
1	2	3	4	5

Note: Average all category scores from the Radar Graph then divide by 7. Circle appropriate average score number in Score Profile Bar above and refer to the Corporate Sustainability Scoring Profiles Section in Chapter 1 for individual Category score descriptions.

Organization: _____

Employees Involved: _____

Date: _____

B Corporate Sustainability Benchmarking Process

Corporate Sustainability Benchmarking Process

Place a check next to each step completed.

Benchmarking Team Formation

_____ 1. Form a corporate sustainability benchmarking team.

_____ 2. Identify corporate sustainability processes within the organization that need to improve.

_____ 3. List in priority order corporate sustainability processes that offer the greatest opportunity for improvement.

_____ 4. Select corporate sustainability processes from the prioritized list.

_____ 5. Develop a list of organizations that are known for corporate sustainability best practices regarding the identified processes.

_____ 6. Reach a consensus on a maximum of three organizations to consider for a benchmark visit (Form 2).

_____ 7. Mail out, e-mail, or fax benchmarking surveys to organizations identified by the team as exhibiting best practices (use *Benchmarking Survey*).

_____ 8. Team collects benchmarking survey data (collect data on Form 1).

_____ 9. Team reaches a consensus on survey scores.

_____ 10. Record survey scores on graphs (top half of Form 2).

_____ 11. Select benchmarking visits based on graph comparisons (minimum of three).

Forms can be downloaded from the CD-ROM located inside the back cover of this book.

Benchmarking Site Visit

_____ 12. Team leader sends a formal letter requesting a site visit (request no more than a three-hour visit).

_____ 13. Send site visit questions with the letter requesting a site visit (base questions on benchmarking survey).

_____ 14. Request in advance any information that the host organization would like to secure from the visiting organization (all approvals must be secured from senior leadership before the site visit is made).

_____ 15. Select two or three team members for each site visit.

_____ 16. After all site visits have been approved, secure travel and accommodations for team members at each site.

_____ 17. Collect and place all pamphlets, handouts, and data received from site visit into a benchmarking folder. All findings are to be shared back onsite with the entire team.

_____ 18. Team leader sends a thank you letter to the host organization that was benchmarked.

Benchmarking Site Visit Completed

_____ 19. Review all data collected from each site visit.

_____ 20. List key findings from each site visit (*Site Visit Benchmarking Overview*, Form 3).

_____ 21. Review and reach a consensus on site visit findings.

_____ 22. Incorporate findings into process improvement (*Benchmark and Process Improvement Steps*, Form 4).

Form 1: Benchmarking Survey

Name of Organization: _____   Date of Phone Call/E-mail: _____

Name/Title of Person Interviewed: _____

This telephone or e-mail survey includes a series of questions to help the benchmark team determine which identified best practice site to visit. The highest possible score achievable by an organization is 50 points. Write the comments in the space provided, then rate the answer.

Rating Scale

Do
Not   World
Know   Class   Best Practice to be Benchmarked _____

1   2   3   4   5   Do you consider your corporate sustainability processes the *best practice* within your in-
                    dustry? Why or why not? _____
                    _____

1   2   3   4   5   Would you rate your corporate sustainability processes against competitors' organiza-
                    tions as being excellent, good, or fair? _____ Why? _____
                    _____

1   2   3   4   5   How does your organization determine that your corporate sustainability processes are
                    best practice within your industry? _____
                    _____

1   2   3   4   5   Does your organization collect corporate sustainability process results? _____
                    Will you share your results? _____

1   2   3   4   5   Have other organizations benchmarked your corporate sustainability processes? _____
                    _____

1   2   3   4   5   How often are your corporate sustainability processes reviewed and benchmarked against
                    other identified best practices inside or outside your organization? _____
                    _____

1   2   3   4   5   Does your organization maintain a budget for your corporate sustainability processes?
                    _____

1   2   3   4   5   How many employees are involved in maintaining your corporate sustainability
                    processes? _____
                    _____

1   2   3   4   5   How do your corporate sustainability processes contribute to increasing overall competi-
                    tiveness for your organization? _____
                    _____

1   2   3   4   5   What impact do your corporate sustainability processes have on your overall organiza-
                    tional effectiveness? _____
                    _____

☐ Total Points

Form 2: Benchmarking Survey Results Graph

(Organization Name)

(Questions)

	1	2	3	4	5	6	7	8	9	10
World class	5									
	4									
	3									
	2									
Not done	1									

Points _____

(Organization Name)

(Questions)

	1	2	3	4	5	6	7	8	9	10
World class	5									
	4									
	3									
	2									
Not done	1									

Points _____

(Organization Name)

(Questions)

	1	2	3	4	5	6	7	8	9	10
World class	5									
	4									
	3									
	2									
Not done	1									

Points _____

Note: Place a dot under each survey question number that best reflects the score from the survey (Form 1). Draw a line to connect the dots.

SITE VISIT SELECTIONS

(Based on benchmarking survey results)

Organization _____   Team Leader _____

Location _____   Team Members _____

Date _____   _____

Organization _____   Team Leader _____

Location _____   Team Members _____

Date _____   _____

Organization _____   Team Leader _____

Location _____   Team Members _____

Date _____   _____

Form 3: Site Visit Benchmarking Overview

Process Benchmarked _____

Organization Location _____

Date _____

Key Findings _____

_____

_____

_____

_____

Process Benchmarked _____

Organization Location _____

Date _____

Key Findings _____

_____

_____

_____

_____

Process Benchmarked _____

Organization Location _____

Date _____

Key Findings _____

_____

_____

_____

Form 4: Benchmarked Process Improvement Steps

Process Benchmarked: _____

Organization Benchmarked: _____

Proposed steps to be incorporated into an improved process based on site visits. Use one form for each sustainability process identified for improvement.

	Process Steps (Present)	Process Steps (Based on site visits)	Process Steps (Improved)
1			
2			
3			
4			
5			
6			
7			
8			
9			
10			

Checklist for 100 Corporate Sustainability Considerations to Benchmark

_____ 1. Review product labeling.

_____ 2. Review supply chain management.

_____ 3. Reduce waste and toxins in supply chain management.

_____ 4. Review web interface.

_____ 5. Review process design and manufacture of goods.

_____ 6. Reduce energy consumption.

_____ 7. Conduct a clean energy review.

_____ 8. Ensure new buildings follow Leadership in Energy and Environmental Design (LEED) standards for future development.

_____ 9. Develop green marketing plan.

_____ 10. Ensure sustainable design in products/services.

_____ 11. Develop green building spaces and communities.

_____ 12. Review recycled product opportunities.

_____ 13. Ensure disposal of spent computers.

_____ 14. Develop equipment maintenance schedules.

_____ 15. Ensure conservation of key corporate resources.

_____ 16. Develop clean technologies.

_____ 17. Review new battery technologies.

_____ 18. Develop improved product disposal methods.

_____ 19. Consider turning out the lights.

_____ 20. Develop emission reductions.

_____ 21. Promote reduction in corporate air travel for employees.

_____ 22. Reduce corporate paper usage.

_____ 23. Reduce customer wait times.

_____ 24. Preserve capital for the organization.

_____ 25. Identify process and product re-engineering opportunities.

_____ 26. Reduce cycle-time for key product/service deliverables.

_____ 27. Encourage energy-saving measures.

_____ 28. Promote increased use of technology to reduce human motion/activity.

_____ 29. Promote efficiency improvements.

_____ 30. Review product changes based on environmental concerns.

_____ 31. Reduce greenhouse gas emissions.

_____ 32. Utilize key suppliers to reduce waste.

_____ 33. Reduce monetary value of regulatory fines.

_____ 34. Reduce worker discrimination.

_____ 35. Improve collective bargaining.

_____ 36. Eliminate child labor.

_____ 37. Eliminate forced or compulsory labor.

_____ 38. Reduce employee turnover.

_____ 39. Improve collective bargaining agreements.

_____ 40. Increase employee training and development.

_____ 41. Define public policy positions.

_____ 42. Conduct a corporate risk analysis.

_____ 43. Reduce incidents of corruption.

_____ 44. Improve product life cycle stages.

_____ 45. Review corporate advertising.

_____ 46. Review corporate policies and procedures.

_____ 47. Reduce corporate pollution.

_____ 48. Develop supplier partnerships.

_____ 49. Review infrastructure investments and/or services provided.

_____ 50. Invest in human capital development.

_____ 51. Identify organization's carbon footprint estimation and reporting.

_____ 52. Improve talent attraction and retention.

_____ 53. Identify and consolidate industry-specific requirements.

_____ 54. Review risk and crisis management initiatives.

_____ 55. Develop a business continuity plan.

_____ 56. Review ethics and compliance issues/concerns.

_____ 57. Identify wind power opportunities.

_____ 58. Identify global temperature concerns.

_____ 59. Reduce carbon emissions.

_____ 60. Identify population concerns as they relate to the environment.

_____ 61. Reduce use of water.

_____ 62. Review solar power opportunities.

_____ 63. Review use of bicycles for corporate use.

_____ 64. Review forest conservation opportunities.

_____ 65. Review wildlife conservation opportunities.

_____ 66. Review ice melting as an indicator of climate change.

_____ 67. Review packaging of products.

_____ 68. Identify cycle-time reduction opportunities.

_____ 69. Ensure data and information accessibility to all employee levels, customers, suppliers, and partners.

_____ 70. Conduct a corporate risk management analysis.

_____ 71. Identify better use of corporate facilities and resources.

_____ 72. Develop a better information management system to ensure better and more efficient access.

_____ 73. Review green certification opportunities.

_____ 74. Develop an environmental purchasing policy.

_____ 75. Conduct employee education and engagement regarding corporate sustainability issues.

_____ 76. Develop a formal corporate sustainability program.

_____ 77. Reduce packaging.

_____ 78. Encourage use of reusable bags.

_____ 79. Reduce shipping container use.

_____ 80. Reduce amount of waste that products contribute to landfills.

_____ 81. Reduce product transportation costs.

_____ 82. Develop quality standards for the organization's products/services and for key suppliers.

_____ 83. Use locally available products, materials, and services.

_____ 84. Improve safe work practices.

_____ 85. Encourage employee involvement in sustainability issues.

_____ 86. Measure key sustainability initiatives.

_____ 87. Budget for corporate sustainability.

_____ 88. Align corporate sustainability initiatives with the organization's strategic plan.

_____ 89. Develop a life cycle analysis to gauge products' overall environmental impact.

_____ 90. Review shipping process and/or practices to ensure timely delivery and cost reductions.

_____ 91. Review janitorial and maintenance use of toxic materials and products.

_____ 92. Cut fuel consumption and usage on corporate vehicles.

_____ 93. Encourage innovation among employees for identification and improvement of key corporate sustainability practices.

_____ 94. Award and recognize employees who promote sustainability throughout the organization and within their neighborhoods and community.

_____ 95. Promote sustainability among employees, customers, and suppliers.

_____ 96. Review new technologies for existing products and services.

_____ 97. Rate _greenness_ of all products purchased.

_____ 98. Lead industry in corporate sustainability efforts.

_____ 99. Save financial resources through better budgeting processes.

_____ 100. Increase market share through sustainable product/service offerings.

D Interviewing Hints and Tips

Interviewing Hints and Tips

DOs

- Be positive when asking questions.
- Allow participants time to formulate answers.
- Make sure questions are understood.
- Reword questions to aid understanding.
- Encourage all participants to answer questions.
- Appear to be interested in all respondents' answers.
- Thank participants for their time.

DON'Ts

- Do not ask questions beyond what the criteria are asking.
- Never read more into the answer than is intended by the question.
- Do not ask rhetorical questions.
- Do not disagree with answers.
- Never be repetitious when asking questions.
- Do not make loaded statements when asking questions.
- Do not allow one participant to monopolize all answers.

Forms can be downloaded from the CD-ROM located inside the back cover of this book.

Corporate Sustainability Assessment Interview Plan and Timetable

Planning Sheet-Date: _____

Assessment Location: _____

Office Phone: _____

Cell Phone: _____

Area Contact Person: _____

Leadership 8:30 a.m.-9:30 a.m.	Strategic Planning 9:35 a.m.-10:35 a.m.	Customer Focus 10:40 a.m.-11:40 a.m.	Measurement, Analysis, and Knowledge Mgt. 11:45 a.m.-12:45 p.m.	Workforce Focus 12:50 p.m.-1:50 p.m.	Process Management 1:55 p.m.-2:55 p.m.	Results 3:00 p.m.-4:00 p.m.
• Executive Level	• Executive Level	• Executive Level	• Executive Level	• Executive Level	• Executive Level	• Executive Level
NAME ___ Position ___	NAME ___ Position ___	NAME ___ Position ___	NAME ___ Position ___	NAME ___ Position ___	NAME ___ Position ___	NAME ___ Position ___
NAME ___ Position ___	NAME ___ Position ___	NAME ___ Position ___	NAME ___ Position ___	NAME ___ Position ___	NAME ___ Position ___	NAME ___ Position ___
NAME ___ Position ___	NAME ___ Position ___	NAME ___ Position ___	NAME ___ Position ___	NAME ___ Position ___	NAME ___ Position ___	NAME ___ Position ___
• Middle Management	• Middle Management	• Middle Management	• Middle Management	• Middle Management	• Middle Management	• Middle Management
NAME ___ Position ___	NAME ___ Position ___	NAME ___ Position ___	NAME ___ Position ___	NAME ___ Position ___	NAME ___ Position ___	NAME ___ Position ___
NAME ___ Position ___	NAME ___ Position ___	NAME ___ Position ___	NAME ___ Position ___	NAME ___ Position ___	NAME ___ Position ___	NAME ___ Position ___
NAME ___ Position ___	NAME ___ Position ___	NAME ___ Position ___	NAME ___ Position ___	NAME ___ Position ___	NAME ___ Position ___	NAME ___ Position ___
• Frontline Staff	• Frontline Staff	• Frontline Staff	• Frontline Staff	• Frontline Staff	• Frontline Staff	• Frontline Staff
NAME ___ Position ___	NAME ___ Position ___	NAME ___ Position ___	NAME ___ Position ___	NAME ___ Position ___	NAME ___ Position ___	NAME ___ Position ___
NAME ___ Position ___	NAME ___ Position ___	NAME ___ Position ___	NAME ___ Position ___	NAME ___ Position ___	NAME ___ Position ___	NAME ___ Position ___
NAME ___ Position ___	NAME ___ Position ___	NAME ___ Position ___	NAME ___ Position ___	NAME ___ Position ___	NAME ___ Position ___	NAME ___ Position ___

E Corporate Sustainability Documentation List

Document Description	Document Date	Revision Date	Document Location	Document Owner

Forms can be downloaded from the CD-ROM located inside the back cover of this book.

F

Corporate Green Sustainability Index (CGSI)[18]

Note: Review all corporate sustainability initiatives and score percent complete and document site locations for your organization.

 Forms can be downloaded from the CD-ROM located inside the back cover of this book.

Corporate Green Sustainability Index (CGSI)

Sustainability Status Legend

Complete Information:	●●
Partial Information:	●○
No Information:	○○

Corporate Sustainability Initiatives		Sustainability Dimensions	Sustainability Status	Where to Find Sustainability Initiatives (Document Site Location)	Total Points Possible (A)	Percent Complete 0–100% 10% units (B)	Corporate Green Sustainability Index (A × B) = C
1.1 Senior Leadership	Vision, Mission, and Values	Economic	○○		70	____ %	
	Legal/Ethical Behavior	Environmental	○○				
	Commitment to Social Issues	Social	○○				
1.2 Governance and Societal Responsibilities	Community Investments	Economic	○○		50	____ %	
	Environmental Plan	Environmental	○○				
	Diversity Plan	Social	○○				
2.1 Strategy Development	Financial Plan and Budget	Economic	○○		40	____ %	
	Environmental Plan	Environmental	○○				
	Human Resource Plan	Social	○○				
2.2 Strategy Deployment	Economic Action Plans	Economic	○○		45	____ %	
	Environmental Action Plans	Environmental	○○				
	Social Issues Action Plans	Social	○○				
3.1 Customer Engagement	Market Analysis	Economic	○○		40	____ %	
	Environmental Issues Identified for Customers	Environmental	○○				
	Customer Concerns Addressed	Social	○○				
3.2 Voice of the Customer	Customer Engagement	Economic	○○		45	____ %	
	Environmental Planning	Environmental	○○				
	Customer Issues Surveyed/Analyzed	Social	○○				
4.1 Measurement, Analysis, and Improvement of Organizational Performance	Financial Performance Data	Economic	○○		45	____ %	
	Environmental Data	Environmental	○○				
	Workforce Performance Data	Social	○○				

Category	Item	Dimension		Score	%
4.2 Management of Information, Knowledge, and Information Technology	Risk Management Data	Economic	○ ○		
	Conservation/Recycling Data	Environmental	○ ○	45	___%
	Best Practice Knowledge/ Benchmark Data	Social	○ ○		
5.1 Workforce Engagement	Productivity Plans	Economic	○ ○		
	Ethical Practices Addressed	Environmental	○ ○	45	___%
	Training & Development	Social	○ ○		
5.2 Workforce Environment	Succession Planning	Economic	○ ○		
	Workforce Environmental Factors Addressed	Environmental	○ ○	40	___%
	Cultural Diversity Addressed	Social	○ ○		
6.1 Work Systems	Work Systems Review(s)	Economic	○ ○		
	Emergency Readiness Plan	Environmental	○ ○	35	___%
	Work Systems Re-engineering Efforts Documented	Social	○ ○		
6.2 Work Processes	Work Systems Design	Economic	○ ○		
	Environmental Purchasing Plan	Environmental	○ ○	50	___%
	Workflow Analysis	Social	○ ○		
7.1 Product Outcomes	Market Results	Economic	○ ○		
	Customer/Supplier Results	Environmental	○ ○	100	___%
	Corporate Results	Social	○ ○		
7.2 Customer-focused Outcomes	Customer Satisfaction Results	Economic	○ ○		
	Environmental Policy Change Results	Environmental	○ ○	70	___%
	Industry Benchmark Results	Social	○ ○		
7.3 Financial and Market Outcomes	Dashboard Indicators	Economic	○ ○		
	Risk Management Results	Environmental	○ ○	70	___%
	Financial/Market Trends	Social	○ ○		

Corporate Green Sustainability Index (CGSI) (Cont.)

Sustainability Status Legend
- Complete Information: ●●
- Partial Information: ●○
- No Information: ○○

	Corporate Sustainability Initiatives	Sustainability Dimensions	Sustainability Status	Where to Find Sustainability Initiatives (Document Site Location)	Total Points Possible (A)	Percent Complete 0-100% 10% units (B)	Corporate Green Sustainability Index (A × B) = C
7.4 Workforce-focused Outcomes	Staff and Leader Development Results	Economic	○○		70	____ %	
	Training and Safety Results	Environmental	○○				
	Workforce Climate Results	Social	○○				
7.5 Process Effectiveness Outcomes	Productivity Results	Economic	○○		70	____ %	
	Business Continuity/Preparedness Results	Environmental	○○				
	Process Innovation Results	Social	○○				
7.6 Leadership Outcomes	Community Support Results	Economic	○○		70	____ %	
	Environmental Results	Environmental	○○				
	Corporate Governance Results	Social	○○				

TOTAL INDEX POINTS 1,000

_____ CGSI Score

After a corporate sustainability assessment of the organization has been completed the assessment team may consider utilizing the above Corporate Green Sustainability Index (CGSI). This Index can be used to help identify and further validate the overall score(s) given to the organization on the Corporate Sustainability Score Sheet that appears at the end of Chapter 9.

The use of the CGSI Index will help an organization to better identify their economic, environmental, and social sustainability dimensions before attempting to complete the Global Reporting Initiative (GRI) Index that appears in Appendix G.

Index Score Profiles

Corporate Green Sustainability Index (CGSI)

DISTRIBUTION OF WRITTEN SCORES	
Range	Common Characteristics
0-125	Very early stages of developing approaches to addressing some basic corporate sustainability planning issues.
126-250	Early stages in the implementation of approaches. Important gaps exist in most categories for corporate sustainability planning and implementation.
251-400	Beginning of a systematic approach, but major gaps exist in approach and deployment in some categories. Early stages of obtaining results stemming from approaches in organization's corporate sustainability planning and implementation.
401-600	Effective approaches and good results in most categories, but deployment in some key areas is still too early to demonstrate results. Further deployment measures and results are needed to demonstrate integration, continuity, and maturity in corporate sustainability, planning, and implementation.
601-750	Refined approaches, including key measures, good deployment, and good results in most categories. Some outstanding activities and results clearly demonstrated. Good evidence of continuity and maturity in key areas. Basis of further deployment and integration is in place. May be an industry leader in corporate sustainability, planning, and implementation.
751-875	Refined approaches, excellent deployment, and good to excellent improvement and levels demonstrated in all categories, good to excellent integration. Industry leaders and a national model in corporate sustainability planning.
875-1000	Outstanding approaches, full deployment, excellent and sustained results. Excellent integration and maturity. National and world leadership in corporate sustainability planning and implementation.

Note: The above Corporate Green Sustainability Index score ranges can be used to gauge an organization's overall progress and maturity in corporate sustainability planning and implementation.

Global Reporting Initiative (GRI) Index[21]

The following is reprinted with permission from Global Reporting Initiative (2006) Sustainability Reporting Guidelines.

The Purpose of a Sustainability Report

Sustainability reporting is the practice of measuring, disclosing and being accountable to internal and external stakeholders for organizational performance towards the goal of sustainable development. 'Sustainability reporting' is a broad term considered synonymous with others used to describe reporting on economic, environmental, and social impacts (e.g., triple bottom line, corporate responsibility reporting, etc.).

A sustainability report should provide a balanced and reasonable representation of the sustainability performance of a reporting organization—including both positive and negative contributions.

Sustainability reports based on the GRI Reporting Framework disclose outcomes and the results that occurred within the reporting period in the content of the organization's commitments, strategy, and management approach. Reports can be used for the following purposes, among others:

- Benchmarking and assessing sustainability performance with respect to laws, norms, codes, performance standards, and voluntary initiatives;
- Demonstrating how the organization influences and is influenced by expectations about sustainable development; and
- Comparing performance within an organization and between different organizations over time.

Orientation to the GRI Reporting Framework

All GRI Reporting Framework documents are developed using a process that seeks consensus through dialogue between stakeholders from business, the investor community, labor, civil society, accounting, academia, and others. All Reporting Framework documents are subject to testing and continuous improvement.

The GRI Reporting Framework is intended to serve as a generally accepted framework for reporting on an organization's economic, environmental, and social performance. It is designed for use by organizations of any size, sector, or location. It takes into account the practical considerations faced by a diverse range of organizations —from small enterprises to those with extensive and geographically dispersed operations. The GRI Reporting Framework contains general and sector-specific content that has been agreed by a wide range of stakeholders around the world to be generally applicable for reporting an organization's sustainability performance.

The Sustainability Reporting Guidelines (the Guidelines) consist of Principles for defining report content and ensuring the quality of reported information.

Global Reporting Initiative (GRI) Index[22]

The Global Reporting Initiative (GRI) Guidelines are an international standard in sustainability reporting which created the GRI reporting framework, known as the GRI Index, the most widely accepted global standard for corporate sustainability reporting, which helps organizations gauge performance against key GRI indicators. For more information about GRI, go to www.globalreporting.org.

Forms can be downloaded from the CD-ROM located inside the back cover of this book.

Core indicators	Covered in Report	Covered in website	Not included	Not reported	Not material*	Not applicable	Not available	List report, program, item, or process	Sustainability Status	

Sustainability Legend — Status

Complete Information	⊙ ⊙
Partial Information	⊙ ○
No Information	○ ○

Core indicators	Covered in Report	Covered in website	Not included	Not reported	Not material*	Not applicable	Not available	List report, program, item, or process	Sustainability Status	
Vision and strategy, profile, governance structure and management systems										
1. Strategy and analysis										
1.1 Statement from the most senior decision-maker of the organization (e.g., CEO, Chair, or equivalent senior position)	x	x						*CEO letter (Example)*	⊙	⊙
1.2 Description of key impacts, risks and opportunities									○	○
2. Organizational profile										
2.1 Name of the organization									○	○
2.2 Primary brands, products, and/or services									○	○
2.3 Operational structure of the organization, including main divisions, operating companies, subsidiaries and joint ventures									○	○
2.4 Location of organization's headquarters									○	○
2.5 Number of countries where the organization operates, and names of countries with either major operations or that are specifically relevant to the sustainability issues covered in the report									○	○
2.6 Nature of ownership and legal form									○	○
2.7 Markets served (including geographic breakdown, sectors served and types of customers/beneficiaries)									○	○
2.8 Scale of the reporting organization (e.g., number of employees, total assets, net sales, quantity of products/services)									○	○
2.9 Significant changes during the reporting period regarding size, structure, or ownership									○	○
2.10 Awards received in the reporting period									○	○

* Not material means lacking substance

Core indicators	Covered in Report	Covered in website	Not included	Not reported	Not material*	Not applicable	Not available	List report, program, item, or process	Sustainability Status
3. Report parameters									
3.1 Reporting period (e.g., fiscal/ calendar year) for information provided									○ ○
3.2 Date of most recent report (if any)									○ ○
3.3 Reporting cycle (annual, biennial, etc.)									
3.4 Contact point for questions regarding the report or its contents									○ ○
3.5 Process for defining report content (e.g., determine materiality, prioritizing topics, and identifying stakeholders)									○ ○
3.6 Boundary of the report (e.g., countries, divisions, subsidiaries, leased facilities, joint ventures, suppliers)									○ ○
3.7 State any specific limitations on the scope or boundary of the report									○ ○
3.8 Basis for reporting on joint ventures, subsidiaries, leased facilities, outsourced operations, and other entities that can significantly affect comparability from period to period and/or between organizations									○ ○
3.9 Data measurement techniques and the bases of calculations, including assumptions and techniques underlying estimations applied to the compilation of the indicators and other information in the report. Explain any decisions not to apply, or to substantially diverge from, the GRI Indicator Protocols									○ ○

* Not material means lacking substance

Core indicators	Covered in Report	Covered in website	Not included	Not reported	Not material*	Not applicable	Not available	List report, program, item, or process	Sustainability Status
3.10 Explanation of the effect of any re-statements of information provided in earlier reports, and the reasons for such re-statement (e.g., mergers/acquisitions, change of base years/ periods, nature of business, measurement methods)									○ ○
3.11 Significant changes from previous reporting periods in the scope, boundary or measurement methods applied in the report									○ ○
3.12 Table identifying the location of the Standard Disclosures in the report									○ ○
3.13 Policy and current practice with regard to seeking external assurance for the report									○ ○
4. Governance, commitments and engagement									
4.1 Governance structure of the organization, including committees under the highest governance body responsible for specific tasks, such as setting strategy or organizational oversight									○ ○
4.2 Indicate whether the Chair of the highest governance body is also an executive officer									○ ○
4.3 For organizations that have a unitary board structure, state the number of members of the highest governance body that are independent and/or non-executive members									
4.4 Mechanisms for shareholders and employees to provide recommendations or direction to the highest governance body									○ ○

* Not material means lacking substance

Core indicators		Covered in Report	Covered in website	Not included	Not reported	Not material*	Not applicable	Not available	List report, program, item, or process	Sustainability Status
4.5	Linkage between compensation for members of the highest governance body, senior managers and executives (including departure arrangements), and the organization's performance (including social and environmental performance)									○ ○
4.6	Processes in place for the highest governance body to ensure conflicts of interest are avoided									○ ○
4.7	Process for determining the qualifications and expertise of the members of the highest governance body for guiding the organization's strategy on economic, environmental and social topics									○ ○
4.8	Internally developed statements of mission or values, codes of conduct, and principles, relevant to economic, environmental and social performance, and the status of their implementation									○ ○
4.9	Procedures of the highest governance body for overseeing the organization's identification and management of economic, environmental and social performance, including relevant risks and opportunities, and adherence or compliance with internationally agreed standards, codes of conduct and principles									○ ○
4.10	Processes for evaluating the highest governance body's own performance, particularly with respect to economic, environmental and social performance									○ ○
4.11	Explanation of whether and how the precautionary approach or principle is addressed by the organization									○ ○

* Not material means lacking substance

Core indicators	Covered in Report	Covered in website	Not included	Not reported	Not material*	Not applicable	Not available	List report, program, item, or process	Sustainability Status
4.12 Externally developed economic, environmental and social charters, principles or other initiatives to which the organization subscribes or endorses									○ ○
4.13 Memberships in associations (such as industry associations) and/or national/international advocacy organizations in which the organization has: Positions in governance bodies; Participates in projects or committees; Provides substantive funding beyond routine membership dues; or Views membership as strategic									○ ○
4.14 List of stakeholder groups engaged by the organization (e.g., communities, customers, suppliers, shareholders, employees)									○ ○
4.15 Basis for identification and selection of stakeholders with whom to engage									○ ○
4.16 Approaches to stakeholder engagement, including frequency of engagement by type and by stakeholder group									○ ○
4.17 Key topics and concerns that have been raised through stakeholder engagement, and how the organization has responded to those key topics and concerns, including through its reporting									○ ○

* Not material means lacking substance

Core indicators	Covered in Report	Covered in website	Not included	Not reported	Not material*	Not applicable	Not available	List report, program, item, or process	Sustainability Status
5. **Management Approach and Performance Indicators**									
Economic Performance Indicators									
Aspect: Economic Performance									
EC1 Direct economic value generated and distributed, including revenues, operating costs, employee compensation, donations and other community investments, retained earnings and payments to capital providers and governments									○ ○
EC2 Financial implications and other risks and opportunities for the organization's activities due to climate change									○ ○
EC3 Coverage of the organization's defined benefit plan obligations									○ ○
EC4 Significant financial assistance received from government									○ ○
Aspect: Market Presence									
EC5 Range of ratios of standard entry level wage compared to local minimum wage at significant locations of operation									○ ○
EC6 Policy, practices and proportion of spending on locally based suppliers at significant locations of operation									○ ○
EC7 Procedures for local hiring and proportion of senior management hired from the local community at significant locations of operation									○ ○

ECONOMIC DIMENSION

* Not material means lacking substance

Core indicators	Covered in Report	Covered in website	Not included	Not reported	Not material*	Not applicable	Not available	List report, program, item, or process	Sustainability Status
ECONOMIC DIMENSION									
Aspect: Indirect Economic Impacts									
EC8 Development and impact of infrastructure investments and services provided primarily for public benefit through commercial, in-kind or pro bono engagement									○ ○
EC9 Understanding and describing significant indirect economic impacts, including the extent of impacts									○ ○
Environmental Performance Indicators									
ENVIRONMENTAL DIMENSION									
Aspect: Materials									
EN1 Materials used by weight or volume									○ ○
EN2 Percentage of materials used that are recycled input materials									○ ○
Aspect: Energy									
EN3 Direct energy consumption by primary energy source									○ ○
EN4 Indirect energy consumption by primary source									○ ○
EN5 Energy saved due to conservation and efficiency improvements									○ ○
EN6 Initiatives to provide energy-efficient or renewable energy-based products and services, and reductions in energy requirements as a result of these initiatives									○ ○
EN7 Initiatives to reduce indirect energy consumption and reductions achieved									○ ○

* Not material means lacking substance

	Core indicators	Covered in Report	Covered in website	Not included	Not reported	Not material*	Not applicable	Not available	List report, program, item, or process	Sustainability Status
ENVIRONMENTAL DIMENSION	**Aspect: Water**									
	EN8 Total water withdrawal by source									○ ○
	EN9 Water sources significantly affected by withdrawal of water									○ ○
	EN10 Percentage and total volume of water recycled and reused									○ ○
	Aspect: Biodiversity									
	EN11 Location and size of land owned, leased, managed in or adjacent to protected areas and areas of high biodiversity value outside protected areas									○ ○
	EN12 Description of significant impacts of activities, products, and services on biodiversity in protected areas and areas of high biodiversity value outside protected areas									○ ○
	EN13 Habitats protected or restored									○ ○
	EN14 Strategies, current actions, and future plans for managing impacts on biodiversity									○ ○
	EN15 Number of IUCN Red List species and national conservation list species with habitats in areas affected by operations, by level of extinction risk									○ ○
	EN16 Total direct and indirect greenhouse gas emissions by weight									○ ○

* Not material means lacking substance

	Core indicators	Covered in Report	Covered in website	Not included	Not reported	Not material*	Not applicable	Not available	List report, program, item, or process	Sustainability Status
ENVIRONMENTAL DIMENSION	**Aspect: Emissions, Effluents, and Waste**									
	EN17 Other relevant indirect greenhouse gas emissions by weight									○ ○
	EN18 Initiatives to reduce greenhouse gas emissions and reductions achieved									○ ○
	EN19 Emissions of ozone-depleting substances by weight									○ ○
	EN20 NO, SO, and other significant air emissions by type and weight									○ ○
	EN21 Total water discharge by quality and destination									○ ○
	EN22 Total weight of waste by type and disposal method									○ ○
	EN23 Total number and volume of significant spills									○ ○
	EN24 Weight of transported, imported, exported, or treated waste deemed hazardous under the terms of the Basel Convention Annex I, II, III, and VIII, and percentage of transported waste shipped internationally									○ ○
	EN25 Identity, size, protected status, and biodiversity value of water bodies and related habitats significantly affected by the reporting organization's discharges of water and runoff									○ ○

* Not material means lacking substance

Core indicators	Covered in Report	Covered in website	Not included	Not reported	Not material*	Not applicable	Not available	List report, program, item, or process	Sustainability Status
ENVIRONMENTAL DIMENSION									
Aspect: Products and Services									
EN26 Initiatives to mitigate environmental impacts of products and services, and extent of impact mitigation									○ ○
EN27 Percentage of products sold and their packaging materials that are reclaimed by category									○ ○
Aspect: Compliance									
EN28 Monetary value of significant fine and total number of non-monetary sanctions for non-compliance with environmental laws and regulations									○ ○
Aspect: Transport									
EN29 Significant environmental impacts of transporting products and other goods and materials used for the organization's operations, and transporting members of the workforce									○ ○
Aspect: Overall									○ ○
EN30 Total environmental protection expenditures and investments by type									○ ○
Social Performance Indicators									
SOCIAL DIMENSION — Aspect: Labor practices and decent work									
LA1 Total workforce by employment type, employment contract, and region									○ ○
LA2 Total number and rate of employee turnover by age group, gender and region									○ ○

* Not material means lacking substance

	Core indicators	Covered in Report	Covered in website	Not included	Not reported	Not material*	Not applicable	Not available	List report, program, item, or process	Sustainability Status
SOCIAL DIMENSION	**Aspect: Labor practices and decent work**									
	LA3 Benefits provided to full-time employees that are not provided to temporary or part-time employees, by major operations									○ ○
	Aspect: Labor/Management Relations									
	LA4 Percentage of employees covered by collective bargaining agreements									○ ○
	LA5 Minimum notice period(s) regarding operational changes, including whether it is specified in collective agreements									○ ○
	Aspect: Occupational Health and Safety									
	LA6 Percentage of total workforce represented in formal joint management-worker health and safety committees that help monitor and advise on occupational health and safety programs									○ ○
	LA7 Rates of injury, occupational diseases, lost days and absenteeism, and number of work-related fatalities by region									○ ○
	LA8 Education, training, counseling, prevention and risk-control programs in place to assist workforce members, their families or community members regarding serious diseases									○ ○
	LA9 Health and safety topics covered in formal agreements with trade unions									○ ○

* Not material means lacking substance

Core indicators	Covered in Report	Covered in website	Not included	Not reported	Not material*	Not applicable	Not available	List report, program, item, or process	Sustainability Status
SOCIAL DIMENSION									
Aspect: Training and Education									
LA10 Average hours of training per year per employee by employee category									○ ○
LA11 Programs for skills management and lifelong learning that support the continued employability of employees and assist them in managing career endings									○ ○
LA12 Percentage of employees receiving regular performance and career development reviews									○ ○
Aspect: Diversity and Equal Employment									
LA13 Composition of governance bodies and breakdown of employees per category according to gender, age group, minority group membership, and other indicators of diversity									○ ○
LA14 Ratio of basic salary of men to women by employee category									○ ○
Human Rights Performance Indicators									
Aspect: Investment and Procurement Practices									
HR1 Percentage and total number of significant investment agreements that include human rights clauses or that have undergone human rights screening									○ ○
HR2 Percentage of significant suppliers and contractors that have undergone screening on human rights and actions taken									○ ○

* Not material means lacking substance

	Core indicators	Covered in Report	Covered in website	Not included	Not reported	Not material*	Not applicable	Not available	List report, program, item, or process	Sustainability Status
SOCIAL DIMENSION	HR3 Total hours of employee training on policies and procedures concerning aspects of human rights that are relevant to operations, including the percentage of employees trained									○ ○
	Aspect: Non-Discrimination									
	HR4 Total number of incidents of discrimination and actions taken									○ ○
	Aspect: Freedom of Association and Collective Bargaining									
	HR5 Operations identified in which the right to exercise freedom of association and collective bargaining may be at significant risk, and actions taken to support these rights									○ ○
	Aspect: Child Labor									
	HR6 Operations identified as having significant risk for incidents of child labor, and measures taken to contribute to the elimination of child labor									○ ○
	Aspect: Forced and Compulsory Labor									
	HR7 Operations identified as having significant risk for incidents of forced or compulsory labor, and measures to contribute to the elimination of forced or compulsory labor									○ ○
	Aspect: Security Practices									
	HR8 Percentage of security personnel trained in the organization's policies or procedures concerning aspects of human rights that are relevant to operations									○ ○

* Not material means lacking substance

Core indicators	Covered in Report	Covered in website	Not included	Not reported	Not material*	Not applicable	Not available	List report, program, item, or process	Sustainability Status
Society Performance Indicators									
Aspect: Indigenous Rights									
HR9 Total number of incidents of violations involving rights of indigenous people and actions taken									○ ○
Aspect: Community									
SO1 Nature, scope, and effectiveness of any programs and practices that assess and manage the impacts of operations on communities, including entering, operating, and existing									○ ○
Aspect: Corruption									
SO2 Percentage and total number of business units analyzed for risks related to corruption									○ ○
SO3 Percentage of employees trained in organization's anti-corruption policies and procedures									○ ○
SO4 Actions taken in response to incidents of corruption									○ ○
Aspect: Public Policy									
SO5 Public policy positions and participation in public policy development and lobbying									○ ○
SO6 Total value of financial and in-kind contributions to political parties, politicians, and related institutions by country									○ ○

(Left vertical label: SOCIAL DIMENSION)

* Not material means lacking substance

	Core indicators	Covered in Report	Covered in website	Not included	Not reported	Not material*	Not applicable	Not available	List report, program, item, or process	Sustainability Status
SOCIAL DIMENSION	**Aspect: Anti-Competitive Behavior**									
	SO7 Total number of legal actions for anti-competitive behavior, anti-trust and monopoly practices and their outcomes									○ ○
	Aspect: Compliance									
	SO8 Monetary value of significant fines and total number of non-monetary sanctions for non-compliance with laws and regulations									○ ○
Product Responsibility Indicators										
SOCIAL DIMENSION	**Aspect: Customer Health and Safety**									
	PR1 Life cycle stages in which health and safety impacts of products and services are assessed for improvement, and percentage of significant products and services categories subject to such procedures									○ ○
	PR2 Total number of incidents of non-compliance with regulations and voluntary codes concerning health and safety impacts of products and services, by type of outcomes									○ ○
	Aspect: Product and Service Labeling									
	PR3 Type of product and service information required by procedures, and percentage of significant products and services subject to such information requirements									○ ○
	PR4 Total number of incidents of non-compliance with regulations and voluntary codes concerning product and service information and labeling, by type of outcomes									○ ○

* Not material means lacking substance

	Core indicators	Covered in Report	Covered in website	Not included	Not reported	Not material*	Not applicable	Not available	List report, program, item, or process	Sustainability Status
SOCIAL DIMENSION	PR5 Practices related to customer satisfaction, including results of surveys measuring customer satisfaction									○ ○
	Aspect: Marketing Communications									
	PR6 Programs for adherence to laws, standards and voluntary codes related to marketing communications, including advertising, promotion and sponsorship									○ ○
	PR7 Total number of incidents of non-compliance with regulations and voluntary codes concerning marketing communications, including advertising, promotion, and sponsorship, by type of outcomes									○ ○
	Aspect: Customer Privacy									
	PR8 Total number of substantiated complaints regarding breaches of customer privacy and losses of customer data									○ ○
	Aspect: Compliance									
	PR9 Monetary value of significant fines for non-compliance with laws and regulations concerning the provision and use of products and services									○ ○

* Not material means lacking substance

Note: Use GRI Index results to develop the organization's corporate sustainability plan and place the Index as an appendix to the corporate sustainability report.

GRI - G3 Reporting Levels[23]

The G3 is the "Third Generation" of the GRI's Sustainability Reporting Guidelines. The guidelines were launched in October 2006. The GRI-G3 seeks to continually improve the Guidelines. The G3 build on the G2 Guidelines released in 2002 which in turn are an evolution of the initial Guidelines which were released in 2000. The G3 Guidelines provide universal guidance for reporting on sustainability performance. They are applicable to small companies, large multinationals, public sector, Non-Government Organizations (NGOs) and other types of organizations world-wide.

The report levels listed below are aligned with the Global Reporting Initiative (GRI) G3 Sustainability Reporting Guidelines released in 2006. To locate the reporting level that your organization may select to follow regarding elements and information contained within the GRI Guidelines, use the index below. For a more detailed explanation of the indicators, and to keep current on any changes in the Guidelines visit the GRI website at www.globalreporting.org.

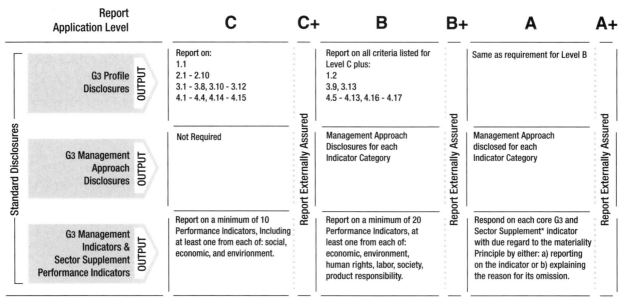

*Sector supplement in final version

Declaring reporting level results in a clear and concise manner regarding which elements of the GRI Reporting Framework have been applied in the presentation of a report will help to meet the needs of new beginners, advanced reporters, and those who are somewhere in between. There are three levels in the GRI-G3 System and they are titled C, B, and A. The reporting criteria found in each level reflect an increase in criteria and performance indicators that need to be addressed from the GRI Reporting Framework. An organization, according to GRI Criteria, can self-declare a "plus" (+) at each level (e.g., C+, B+, A+) if the organization has utilized "qualified" external assistance in reviewing their report. After the GRI Index has been completed, use the results as the foundation for developing the organization's corporate sustainability report.

H Glossaries of Performance Excellence and Sustainability Terms

Performance Excellence Assessment Terms[19]

action plans–refers to specific actions that respond to short- and longer-term strategic objectives.

administrative processes and support services–processes and services that may include activities and operations such as finance and accounting, software services, marketing, public relations, information services, purchasing, personnel, legal services, facilities management, research and development, secretarial, and other administrative services.

alignment–refers to consistency of plans, processes, information, resource decisions, actions, results, and analyses to support key organization-wide goals.

analysis–refers to an examination of facts and data to provide a basis for effective decisions. Analysis often involves the determination of cause-effect relationships.

anecdotal–refers to process information that lacks specific methods, measures, deployment mechanisms, and evaluation, improvement, and learning factors. Anecdotal information frequently uses examples and describes individual activities rather than systematic processes.

approach–refers to the methods used by an organization to address the Baldrige Criteria Item requirements. Approach includes the appropriateness of the methods to the Item requirements and the effectiveness of their use.

Baldrige Assessment–an organizational evaluation based on the seven categories, 18 items, and 89 areas of the Malcolm Baldrige National Quality Award criteria.

basic requirements–refers to the topic Criteria users need to address when responding to the most central concept of an Item.

benchmarking–teams of employees review and visit best practice programs, services, and practices. Benchmarking can include site visits to other organizations and telephone interviews. Benchmarking is an involved process that organizations pursue when seeking to become *world class* in processes that they have identified as needing improvement.

business and support services–includes units and operations involving finance and accounting, software services, sales, marketing, public relations, information services, purchasing and personnel, and so forth.

business ethics–a published statement of values and business ethics that are promoted and practiced both internally and externally by the organization.

business plan–a statement of business plans and strategies that is published and shared throughout an organization. Many organizations when beginning their quality improvement process have a separate business plan and quality plan.

collaborators–refers to those organizations or individuals who cooperate with your organization to support a particular activity or event or who cooperate on an intermittent basis when short-term goals are aligned or are the same. Typically, collaborations do not involve formal agreements or arrangements.

competitive comparisons–an organization's comparison of its products/services against major competitors and industry comparisons.

223

control chart–a graph that is used by employees to determine if their work process is within prescribed limits.

core competencies–refers to your organization's areas of greatest expertise.

cross-functional teams–teams formed from different divisions or departments to solve or create new solutions to an organizational problem or opportunity.

customer–the end-user of all products and services produced within an organization. Customers are both internal and external.

customer contact employee–an employee who has direct interface with external customers, in person, via telephone, or other means.

customer relationship management–an organization's interactions and relationships with its customers.

cycle time–the amount of time it takes to complete a specified work process.

data–the collection of facts, information, or statistics.

data analysis–the breaking apart of data to help the organization gauge improvement.

deployment–refers to the *extent* to which an approach is applied in addressing the requirements of a Baldrige Criteria Item. Deployment is evaluated on the basis of the breadth and depth of application of the approach to relevant work units throughout the organization.

diversity–refers to valuing and benefiting from personal differences. These differences address many variables, including race, religion, color, gender, national origin, disability, sexual orientation, age and generational preferences, education, geographic origin, and skill characteristics, as well as differences in ideas, thinking, academic disciplines, and perspectives.

documented improvement–a process improvement that has been supported against baseline data and documented at measured intervals.

effective–refers to how well a process or a measure addresses its intended purpose. Determining effectiveness requires (1) the evaluation of how well the process is aligned with the organization's needs and how well the process is deployed or (2) the evaluation of the outcome of the measure used.

employee involvement–involvement of employees across the organization at all levels.

employee morale–the attitudes of employees in regard to their willingness to perform work tasks.

empowerment–employees' freedom to respond to customer demands and requests.

ergonomics–the evaluation of an organization's facilities and equipment to ensure compatibility between workers and their work processes.

ethical behavior–refers to how an organization ensures that all its decisions, actions, and stakeholder interactions conform to the organization's moral and professional principles.

flowchart–a graphic map of a work process used by employee teams to document the current condition of a process.

goals and strategies–organizations develop goals and strategies for short-term (1 to 2 years) and long-term (2 years or more) desired results. Goals and strategies are usually written and distributed across the organization.

governance–refers to the system of management and controls exercised in the stewardship of your organization. It includes the responsibilities of your organization's owners/shareholders, board of directors, and senior leaders.

high-performance work–refers to work processes used to systematically pursue ever-higher levels of overall organizational and individual performance, including quality, productivity, innovation rate, and cycle time performance. High-performance work results in improved service for customers and other stakeholders.

improvement plan–a written plan that the organization has published to accomplish desired improvement results.

innovation–refers to making meaningful change to improve products, processes, or organizational effectiveness and to create new value for stakeholders. Innovation involves the adoption of an idea, process, technology, product, or business model that is either new or new to its proposed application.

integration–refers to the harmonization of plans, processes, information, resource decisions, actions, results, and analyses to support key organization-wide goals. Effective integration goes beyond alignment and is achieved when the individual components of a performance management system operate as a fully interconnected unit.

internal customer-supplier network–an organization's employee network; referred to as inside customers and suppliers.

key–refers to the major or most important elements or factors, those that are critical to achieving your intended outcome.

key indicators–key measures of performance (that is, productivity, cycle time, cost, and other effectiveness measures).

knowledge assets–refers to the accumulated intellectual resources of your organization. It is the knowledge possessed by your organization and its workforce in the form of information, ideas, learning, understanding, memory, insights, cognitive and technical skills, and capabilities. Your workforce, software, patents, databases, documents, guides, policies and procedures, and technical drawings are repositories of your organization's knowledge assets. Knowledge assets are held not only by an organization but reside within its customers, suppliers, and partners, as well.

leadership system–refers to how leadership is exercised, formally and informally, throughout the organization; it is the basis for and the way key decisions are made, communicated, and carried out.

learning–refers to new knowledge or skills acquired through evaluation, study, experience, and innovation.

levels–refers to numerical information that places or positions an organization's results and performance on a meaningful measurement scale. Performance levels permit evaluation relative to past performance, projections, goals, and appropriate comparisons.

Malcolm Baldrige National Quality Award for Performance Excellence–an Award that is given by the United States National Institute of Standards and Technology (NIST), an agency of the U.S. Department of Commerce, which manages the Baldrige National Quality Program. The Award was named for Malcolm Baldrige, who served as United States Secretary of Commerce during the Reagan administration from 1981 until his death in 1987. The Award Criteria are designed to help improve organizational performance practices, capabilities, and results. This is the only quality award that is awarded by the President of the United States.

manufacturing organization–an organization that makes or processes raw materials into a finished product.

measurement–the process of gauging an organization's results against its customer requirements.

measures and indicators–refers to numerical information that quantifies input, output, and performance dimensions of processes, products, programs, projects, services, and the overall organization (outcomes). Measures and indicators might be simple (derived from one measurement) or composite.

mission–refers to the overall function of an organization. The mission answers the question, "What is this organization attempting to accomplish?" The mission might define customers or markets served, distinctive or core competencies, or technologies used.

mission statement–many organizations have a published document that defines an organization's reason for existing. The mission statement is shared with employees, suppliers, and customers.

partners–refers to those key organizations or individuals who are working in concert with your organization to achieve a common goal or to improve performance. Typically, partnerships are formal arrangements for a specific aim or purpose, such as to achieve a strategic objective or to deliver a specific product or service.

performance–refers to outputs and their outcomes obtained from processes, products, and customers that permit evaluation and comparison relative to goals, standards, past results, and other organizations. Performance can be expressed in nonfinancial and financial terms.

performance data–results of improvements in product and service production and delivery processes.

performance excellence–refers to an integrated approach to organizational performance management that results in (1) delivery of ever-improving value to customers and stakeholders, contributing to organizational sustainability; (2) improvement of overall organizational effectiveness and capabilities; and (3) organizational and personal learning.

performance projections–refers to estimates of future performance. Projections may be inferred from past performance, may be based on competitors' or similar organizations' performance that must be met or exceeded, may be predicted based on changes in a dynamic environment, or may be goals for future performance.

process–a series of steps linked together to provide a product or service for an end-user.

process control–a control device to detect and remove causes of variation to a defined process.

process management–organization's maintenance of defined processes to ensure that both quality and performance are continuously improved.

productivity–refers to measures of the efficiency of resource use.

productivity improvement–measured reduction in an organization's key operational processes.

problem-solving tools–tools used by teams to solve process problems (that is, flowcharts, Pareto analysis, histograms, control charts, cause-and-effect diagrams, and matrix diagrams).

problem-solving teams–teams of employees selected and empowered by management to assess, analyze, and solve problems within an organization. These teams may be cross-functional, work group, departmental, or project-focused.

public responsibility–an organization's impact and possible impact on society with its products, services, and operations. This includes business ethics, environment, education, health care, community services, and safety as they relate to the public.

quality plan–a written statement of an organization's plan for maintaining and improving quality. An organization that has just begun the quality improvement process usually has this plan separate from its business plan. The more mature organizations in quality usually integrate their quality plan with their business plan.

quality assessment–an assessment of an organization's approach to and implementation of quality.

quality results–an organization's achievement levels and improvement trends.

results–refers to outputs and outcomes achieved by an organization.

safe work practices–an organization's promotion of safety on the worksite for employees. Many organizations have documented guidelines for employees to follow and they collect data on safe work practices.

senior executive–refers to the organization's highest ranking official and those reporting directly to that official.

senior leaders–refers to an organization's senior management group or team.

service organization–non-manufacturing organizations, such as utilities, schools, government, transportation, finance, real estate, restaurants, hotels, news media, business services, professional services, and repair services.

small business–complete businesses with no more than 500 full-time employees. Business activities may include manufacturing and/or service.

stakeholders–refers to all groups that are or might be affected by an organization's actions and success. Examples of key stakeholders might include customers, the workforce, partners, collaborators, governing boards, stockholders, donors, suppliers, taxpayers, regulatory bodies, policy makers, funders, and local and professional communities.

statistical process control (SPC)–technique for measuring and analyzing process variations.

strategic advantages–refers to those marketplace benefits that exert a decisive influence on an organization's likelihood of future success.

strategic challenges–refers to those pressures that exert a decisive influence on an organization's likelihood of future success.

strategic objectives–refers to an organization's articulated aims or responses to address major change or improvement, competitiveness or social issues, and business advantages.

strategic plan–a detailed plan of action developed by an organization establishing and defining measurable goals to achieve continuous quality improvement within the organization. A strategic plan can be broken into short term (1 to 2 years) and long term (more than 2 years).

supplier–an individual or group, either internal to the organization or external, that provides input to a work group or customer.

supplier certification program–a formal supplier program used by an organization to improve supplier quality. Many organizations partner with critical suppliers and establish a relationship of trust and measurable results.

supplier partnership–a supplier process practiced by many service and manufacturing organizations. Organizations establish a preferred supplier program that is based on a trust relationship with measurable results. Supplier partnerships are usually a prelude to a more formalized supplier certification program.

survey process–the means by which an organization collects data from its customers and employees. These surveys may help an organization focus on internal/external customer satisfaction issues.

sustainability–refers to your organization's ability to address current business needs and to have the agility and strategic management to prepare successfully for your future business, market, and operating environment. Sustainability considerations might include workforce capability and capacity, resource availability, technology, knowledge, core competencies, work systems, facilities, and equipment. Sustainability might be affected by changes in the marketplace and customer preferences, changes in the financial markets, and changes in the legal and regulatory environment. In addition, sustainability has a component related to day-to-day preparedness for real-time or short-term emergencies.

system–a set of well-defined and well-designed processes for meeting the organization's quality and performance requirements.

systematic–refers to approaches that are well-ordered, are repeatable, and use data and information so learning is possible. In other words, approaches are systematic if they build in the opportunity for evaluation, improvement, and sharing, thereby permitting a gain in maturity.

targets–desired goals that organizations have in their strategic planning process.

third-party survey–a survey conducted by a resource outside the organization.

Total Quality Management (TQM)–a management philosophy that focuses on continuous quality improvement throughout an organization.

trends–refers to numerical information that shows the direction and rate of change for an organization's results. Trends provide a time sequence of organizational performance. A minimum of three historical (not projected) data points generally is needed to begin to ascertain a trend. More data points are needed to define a statistically valid trend. The time period for a trend is determined by the cycle time of the process being measured.

user-friendly–a process that is understandable to all levels of a workforce within an organization. A user-friendly process can be understood because it is written in simpler, more understandable language.

values statement–a published document that describes an organization's beliefs. This values statement is usually shared with faculty, staff, students, customers, suppliers, and the community.

vision–refers to the desired future state of your organization. The vision describes where the organization is headed, what it intends to be, or how it wishes to be perceived in the future.

vision statement–many organizations have a published document that defines their direction for the next five to 10 years. The vision statement is shared with both internal and external groups.

work processes–refers to your most important internal value creation processes. They might include product design and delivery, customer support, supply chain management, business, and support processes. They are the processes that involve the majority of your organization's workforce and produce customer, stakeholder, and stockholder value. Your key work processes frequently relate to your core competencies, to the factors that determine your success relative to competitors, and to the factors considered important for business growth by your senior leaders.

work systems–refers to how the work of your organization is accomplished. Work systems involve your workforce, your key suppliers and partners, your contractors, your collaborators, and other components of the supply chain needed to produce and deliver your products and your business and support processes.

workforce–refers to all people actively involved in accomplishing the work of your organization, including paid employees (for example, permanent, part-time, temporary, and telecommuting employees, as well as contract employees supervised by the organization) and volunteers, as appropriate. The workforce includes team leaders, supervisors, and managers at all levels.

workforce capability–refers to your organization's ability to accomplish its work processes through the knowledge, skills, abilities, and competencies of its people.

workforce capacity–refers to your organization's ability to ensure sufficient staffing levels to accomplish its work processes and successfully deliver your products to your customers, including the ability to meet seasonal or varying demand levels.

workforce engagement–refers to the extent of workforce commitment, both emotional and intellectual, to accomplishing the work, mission, and vision of the organization. Organizations with high levels of workforce engagement are often characterized by high-performing work environments in which people are motivated to do their utmost for the benefit of their customers and for the success of the organization.

world-class organization–an organization that produces excellent results in major areas with a sound quality management approach to corporate sustainability. This organization is totally integrated with a systematic prevention-based system that is continuously refined through evaluations and improvement cycles.

zero-based organization–an organization that has no system in place for corporate sustainability and is anecdotal in its implementation of a sound, systematic, effective, and management-based approach to corporate sustainability that is fully integrated and implemented across the organization.

Sustainability Terms[20]

accountability–being answerable to all stakeholders, including any natural or social systems affected by a business such as customers, employees, and communities.

appreciative inquiry–a philosophy of organizational assessment and change that seeks examples of success to emulate and organizational or personal strengths to build upon, rather than focusing upon fixing negative or ineffective organizational processes.

best practice–an effective, innovative solution, process, or procedure that demonstrates a business' dedication to making progress in environmental and corporate social responsibility; sometimes shared with collaborators and competitors to shape standards for an industry.

biodiesel–a type of fuel made by combining animal fat or vegetable oil (such as soybean oil or used restaurant grease) with alcohol; biodiesel can be directly substituted for diesel (known as B100, for 100 percent biodiesel), or be used as an additive mixed with traditional diesel (known as B20, for 20 percent bio-diesel).

bioenergy–energy generated from renewable, biological sources (biomass) such as plants, to be used for heat, electricity, or vehicle fuel.

biofuel–fuel created from renewable, biological sources such as plants or animal byproducts, but excluding biological material (such as natural gas, coal, or methane) which has been transformed by geological processes.

biomass–living or recently-dead organic material that can be used as an energy source or in industrial production; excludes organic material that has been transformed by geological processes (such as coal or petroleum).

biomimicry–a science that studies natural processes and models in order to imitate the designs to solve human problems, that is, studying a leaf to better understand and design solar cells.

brown power/energy–electricity generated from the combustion of nonrenewable fossil fuels (coal, oil, or natural gas) which generates significant amounts of greenhouse gases.

brownfield–land previously utilized by commercial or industrial facilities that remains abandoned with known or perceived environmental contamination.

Brundtland Commission–formally known as the World Commission on Environment and Development (WCED), by the name of its Chair Gro Harlem Brundtland, was convened by the United Nations in 1983. The Commission was created to address the growing concern of world-wide environmental problems that were in the common interest of all nations to establish policies for sustainable development.

Calvert–an investment firm that highlights socially responsible investing and publishes an annual index of the largest U.S. companies that represent socially responsible investments.

cap and trade system–a strategy to reduce carbon emissions via financial incentives; *caps* establish emissions limits and fines for exceeding those limits, while companies operating below their carbon limits can sell or *trade* their offsets to companies that are operating above the limits.

carbon dioxide (CO_2)–the greenhouse gas whose concentration is being most affected directly by human activities. CO_2 also serves as the reference to compare all other greenhouse gases. The major source of CO_2 emissions is fossil fuel combustion.

carbon footprint–the total amount of greenhouse gases emitted directly or indirectly through any human activity, typically expressed in equivalent tons of either carbon or carbon dioxide.

carbon trading–a trading system for countries, companies, and individuals designed to offset carbon emissions from one activity with another, whereby those who cannot meet their emissions goals may purchase credits from those who surpass their goals.

cause-related marketing–a business strategy whereby a company aligns its mission and goals to create a specific and tailored partnership with a nonprofit organization or cause.

Ceres–a national network of investors, environmental organizations, and other public interest groups working with companies and investors to address sustainability challenges such as global climate change; Ceres hosts an annual competition to highlight the best examples of sustainability reporting in North America; *pronounced "series"*.

child labor–the practice of employing children under a specified legal minimum age as set by a country or government; more frequently exploited in developing countries in order to establish competitive labor costs.

Clean Air Act–federal legislation passed in 1970 and amended in 1990 that authorizes the EPA to set National Ambient Air Quality Standards and to regulate industry in order to meet those maximum emissions levels.

clean production–a concept developed under the Kyoto Protocol in which manufacturing processes reduce environmental impact and decrease ecological problems by minimizing energy and raw materials use, and making sure emissions and waste are as minimal and as non-toxic to environmental and human health as possible.

Clean Water Act–federal legislation passed in 1972 and amended in 1976 that requires the EPA to set maximum pollutant levels for each known contaminant in U.S. surface waters and authorizes the EPA to regulate industrial discharge in order to meet those standards.

climate change–changes in global climate patterns (such as temperature, precipitation, or wind) that last for extended periods of time as a result of either natural processes or human activity; the contemporary concern is that human activity is now transcending natural processes in causing the most prevalent climate changes of our time.

closed-loop recycling–a process of utilizing a recycled product in the manufacturing of a similar product or the remanufacturing of the same product.

closed-loop supply chain–an ideal in which a supply chain completely reuses, recycles, or composts all wastes generated during production; at minimum *closed-loop supply chain* indicates that the company which produces a good is also responsible for its disposal.

Comprehensive Environmental Response, Compensation, and Liability Act (CERCLA or Superfund)–federal legislation passed in 1980 that established a tax on the petroleum and chemical industries to fund cleanup of hazardous waste sites, as well as establishing EPA authority to assign responsibility for that cleanup to the polluters or purchasers of contaminated land.

corporate citizenship–a company's responsible involvement with the wider community in which it is situated.

corporate health–the idea that companies, especially commercial businesses, have a duty to care for all of their stakeholders in all aspects of their operations.

corporate responsibility report–a periodically-published report of a company's corporate responsibility practices, goals, and progress toward achieving those goals that may be included with the company's annual report or as a separate publication that focuses on the company's social and environmental impact; the process of creating this report is meant to uncover strengths and weaknesses as well as enhance transparency for all company stakeholders.

corporate responsibility–the degree to which companies manage business practices to produce an overall positive impact on society.

corporate social responsibility–the continuing commitment by businesses to behave ethically and contribute to economic development while improving the quality of life of the workplace as well as the local community and society at large; a company's obligation to be accountable to all of its stakeholders in all its operations and activities (including financial stakeholders as well as suppliers, customers, and employees) with the aim of achieving sustainable development not only in the economic dimension but also in the social and environmental dimensions.

corporate sustainability report–a periodic report published by a company to outline its progress toward meeting its financial, environmental, and social sustainability goals; often published in compliance with third-party standards such as the UN Global Compact or Global Reporting Initiative; *see Corporate Responsibility Report*.

cradle-to-cradle–a design philosophy put forth by architect William McDonough that considers the life-cycle of a material or product, and ensures that the product is completely recycled at the end of its defined lifetime.

demand-side management–the implementation of policies that control or influence demand of certain products or services.

dematerialization–the reduction of total materials used in providing customers with products or services.

Domini Social Investment–an investment firm specializing exclusively in socially-responsible investing based on its own development and application of social and environmental standards.

Dow Jones Sustainability Indexes (DJSI)–the first global indexes to track the financial performance of sustainability-driven companies.

eco-effectiveness–designing industrial processes so they do not generate toxic pollution and *waste* in the first place. Long-term prosperity depends on the effectiveness of processes designed to be healthy and renewable in the first place.

eco-efficiency–the creation of more goods and services while using fewer resources and creating less waste and pollution.

eco-friendly–a product, practice, or process that is *green* or good for the environment, creating no unnecessary or hazardous waste and minimizing use of non-renewable, natural resources.

ecological economics–*see natural capital, ethical investments, environmental valuation.*

ecological footprint–the total amount of land, food, water, and other resources used by, or the total ecological impact of, a person or organization's subsistence; usually measured in acres or hectares of productive land.

ecological justice, a.k.a. ecojustice–the concept that all components of an ecosystem (such as plant and animal life as well as natural resources) have a right to be free from human exploitation and free from destruction, discrimination, bias, or extinction; *distinct from environmental justice.*

ECPI Ethical Index Global–selects the top 300 capitalized companies in the global marketplace, which are eligible investments according to a set of defined ethical standards that help ensure sustainability and responsibility in their corporate business practices.

energy efficiency–the result of actions taken to reduce dependence on or to save fuels, that is, selection of road vehicles with higher MPG or the use of renewable sources of power for heating and cooling.

environmental audit–a systematic, documented, periodic, and objective evaluation of how well a project, organization, individual, or service is performing in terms of environmental impact, including, but not necessarily limited to, compliance with any relevant standards or regulations.

environmental cost accounting–costs that may arise as a result of corporate environmental activities—that is, statutory or voluntary activities aimed at avoiding, reducing, treating, and treatment/disposing of corporate waste and emissions—but also as a result of lacking corporate environmental policy.

environmental impact assessment (EIA)–an assessment of potential environmental effects of development projects; required by the National Environmental Policy Act (NEPA) for any proposed major federal action with significant environmental impact.

environmental justice–the concept of equal access to environmental resources and protection from environmental hazards regardless of race, ethnicity, national origin, or income; *distinct from Ecological Justice.*

Environmental Protection Agency (EPA)–EPA is the United States government agency which leads the nation's environmental science, research, education, and assessment efforts. The mission of the Environmental Protection Agency is to protect human health and the environment.

Environmental Risk Assessment (ERA)–the tracking and rating of environmental risks, such as emissions, associated with a product and its manufacturing.

environmental standards–*see standards.*

environmental sustainability–*see sustainability.*

environmental valuation–the inclusion of environmental costs and benefits into accounting practices using such mechanisms as taxes, tax incentives, and subsidies; by quantifying environmentally-related costs and revenues, better management decisions and increased investment in environmental protection and improvement are encouraged.

environmental, social and government (ESG)–an acronym commonly used by investment firms to refer to the types of issues or factors considered in measuring a company's *responsible practices*; these issues or factors include the environmental effects of a company's business practices, social metrics such as fair pay and treatment of labor, and community involvement and ethical corporate governance practices that are both transparent and anti-corruption.

Ethibel Sustainability Index (ESI)–provides a comprehensive perspective on the financial performance of the world's leading companies in terms of sustainability for institutional investors, asset managers, banks, and retail investors.

ethical investments–*see socially responsible investing.*

Ethinvest Environmental Index Australia–an index that measures the top 30 companies that exhibit sustainable business practices in Australia.

Fair Trade–an international trading partnership that seeks to help marginalized producers and workers achieve financial self-sufficiency by establishing direct lines of trade between producers and consumers, guaranteeing producers fair prices for goods, restricting exploitative labor processes, and favoring environmentally-sustainable production processes through a system of labeling products as *fair trade.*

fossil fuels–fuels, such as natural gas, coal, and petroleum, that formed from the fossilized (or geologically transformed) remains of plants and animals.

FTSE4Good Index Series–measures the performance of companies that meet globally recognized corporate sustainability and responsibility standards. The Index is used to facilitate investment in companies that promote and practice corporate sustainability/responsibility business practices.

geothermal energy–a natural and sustainable form of heat energy derived from steam and hot water found below the surface of the Earth.

global climate change–change in the world's climate most often attributed to human influences and activities.

Global 100 Most Sustainable Organizations–a project that recognizes companies who exhibit *best practice* social, environmental and strategic governance initiatives. The annual global winners are announced each year at the World Economic Forum in Davos, Switzerland.

Global Reporting Initiative (GRI)–a reporting standard generally accepted to be the leading international standard for reporting social, environmental, and economic performance.

global warming–the gradual, average increase of temperature of the Earth's near-surface atmosphere that is accelerated by the greenhouse gases emitted by human industry; global warming is one type of and a contributor to other types of global climate change in general, such that at individual locations the temperature may fluctuate or drop even though the global average is rising.

green accounting–the incorporation of the amount of natural resources used and pollutants expelled into conventional economic accounting in order to provide a detailed measure of all environmental consequences of any and all economic activities.

green building–a comprehensive process of design and construction that employs techniques to minimize adverse environmental impacts and reduce the energy consumption of a building, while contributing to the health and productivity of its occupants; a common metric for evaluating green buildings is the LEED (Leadership in Energy and Environmental Design) certification.

green design–the design of products, services, buildings, or experiences that are sensitive to environmental issues and achieve greater efficiency and effectiveness in terms of energy and materials use.

greenhouse effect–the trapping of heat within the Earth's atmosphere by greenhouse gases such as CO_2, which is necessary to keep the planet at a temperature warm enough to sustain life, but becomes dangerous when greenhouse gases produced by humans cause the effect to intensify and push the global temperature to too high a level.

greenhouse gas–a gas that contributes to the natural greenhouse effect, whereby heat is trapped within the Earth's atmosphere, including: carbon dioxide, methane, nitrous oxide, hydrofluorocarbons, perfluorocarbons, and sulfur hexafluoride.

greenwashing–the process by which a company publicly and misleadingly declares itself to be environmentally-friendly but internally participates in environmentally- or socially-unfriendly practices.

Humanix 50 Index Sweden–the Index includes 50 sustainable companies in Sweden that are listed on the Stockholm Stock Exchange that promote social, ethical, and environmental values in their business models.

ISO 9000 and ISO 14000–the International Organization for Standardization (ISO) is a worldwide federation of national standards bodies. ISO 9000 and ISO 14000 are families of standards and guidelines relating to management systems. ISO 9000 is associated with quality management. ISO 14000 is associated with environmental management.

Jantzi Social Index Canada–index that promotes social responsibility in corporate business practices among Canadian companies.

Johannesburg Stock Exchange/FTSE4Good Index South Africa–index that promotes ethical investments in South African companies and is modeled after the London FTSE4Good Index.

Kyoto Protocol–an international agreement reached during a summit in Kyoto, Japan in 1997, the Kyoto Protocol builds upon the United Nations Framework Convention on Climate Change and sets targets and time-tables for industrialized countries to reduce their greenhouse gas emissions; 175 parties have so far ratified the Protocol and are legally bound to adhere to its principles.

LEED Certification–an acronym for Leadership in Energy and Environmental Design sponsored by the United States Green Building Council that creates standards for developing high performance, sustainable buildings.

life cycle assessment (LCA)–a process of evaluating the effects of a product or its designated function on the environment over the entire period of the product's life in order to increase resource-use efficiency and decrease liabilities; commonly referred to as *cradle-to-grave* analysis.

life-cycle design–the identification, characterization, and evaluation of potential environmental impacts throughout the life cycle of a product or service from cradle to grave including reconstruction, use, and disposal.

material taxes–taxes collected from customers on hard-to-dispose of materials by the wholesaler (typically for oil, antifreeze, solvents, and so on).

LOHAS Market–an acronym for Lifestyles of Health and Sustainability; a market that consists of mindful consumers passionate about the environment, sustainability, social issues, and health.

meta-trend–a global and overarching force that will affect many multidimensional changes; for example, environmental impacts on business, individuals, and countries.

natural capital–a company's environmental assets and natural resources existing in the physical environment, either owned (such as mineral, forest, or energy resources) or simply utilized in business operations (such as clean water and atmosphere); often traditional economic measures and indicators fail to take into account the development use of natural capital, although preservation of its quantity and quality and therefore its sustainable use is essential to a business' long-term survival and growth.

natural capitalism–refers to the resources and services provided by nature. They are of enormous economic value—more so than the gross world product. Natural capitalism is a system of four interlinking principles, where business and environmental interests overlap, and in which businesses can better satisfy their customers' needs, increase profits, and help solve environmental problems all at the same time.

nitrogen oxides (NOx)–gases consisting of one molecule of nitrogen and varying numbers of oxygen molecules. Nitrogen oxides are produced in the emissions of vehicle exhausts and from power stations. In the atmosphere, nitrogen oxides can contribute to formation of photochemical ozone (smog), can impair visibility, and have health consequences; they are thus considered pollutants.

non-governmental organization (NGO)–a private, non-profit organization that is independent of business and government, that works toward some specific social, environmental, or economic goal through research, activism, training, promotion, advocacy, lobbying, community service, and so on.

non-renewable resource–a natural resource that is unable to be regenerated or renewed fully and without loss of quality once it is used, that is, fossil fuels or minerals.

open-loop recycling–a recycling process in which materials from old products are made into new products in a manner that changes the inherent properties of the materials, often via a degradation in quality, such as recycling white writing paper into cardboard rather than more premium writing paper; often used for steel, paper, and plastic, open-loop recycling is also known as downcycling or reprocessing.

organic–a term signifying the absence of pesticides, hormones, synthetic fertilizers, and other toxic materials in the cultivation of agricultural products; *organic* is also a food labeling term that denotes the product was produced under the authority of the Organic Foods Production Act.

ozone (O_3)–an important greenhouse gas found in both the stratosphere and the troposphere (*lowest region of the atmosphere*). In the stratosphere, ozone provides a protective layer shielding the Earth from ultraviolet radiation and subsequent harmful health effects on humans and the environment. In the troposphere, oxygen molecules in ozone combine with other chemicals and gases (oxidization) to cause smog.

ozone depletion–stratospheric ozone is necessary to filter out harmful radiation from the sun. Scientists have linked depletion of stratospheric ozone to increased incidence of skin cancer and other disorders and environmental degradation. Under international convention and national laws, governments are prohibiting the production, use, and release of ozone-depleting substances.

particulate matter–tiny pieces of solid or liquid matter, such as soot, dust, fumes, or mist.

people, planet, profit–the expanded set of values for companies and individuals to use in measuring organizational and societal success, specifically economic, environmental, and social values; *people, planet, profit* are also referred to as the components of the *triple bottom line; see triple bottom line.*

product stewardship–recognizes the benefits of combining economic and environmental objectives. By being eco-efficient, goods, and services can be produced with less energy and fewer raw materials, resulting in less waste, less pollution, and less cost. Product stewardship recognizes that product manufacturers can and must take on new responsibilities to reduce the environmental footprint of their products.

renewable energy–energy derived from non-fossil fuel resources (such as solar, wind, or geothermal energy) that can be replenished in full without a loss of quality; separate from sustainable energy because of emissions or other unsustainable impacts of the process of creating renewable energy.

renewable portfolio standard–a state policy that requires the state to meet a certain percentage of its energy needs with renewable energy by a certain date.

renewable resources–natural resources that may be replenished through natural cycles and sound management. The sun, wind, wetlands, forests, and croplands are examples of renewable resources.

responsible practices–business practices that exemplify corporate responsibility; *see corporate responsibility.*

shareholder resolution–a corporate policy recommendation proposed by a shareholder holding at least $2,000 market value or 1 percent of the company's voting shares presented for a vote by other shareholders at the company's annual meeting; an increasing number of shareholder resolutions request a company and/or its board of directors to carry out responsible business practices, especially regarding social, environmental, and human rights issues.

SmartWaySM–the Environmental Protection Agency's (EPA's) SmartWay brand identifies products and services that reduce transportation-related emissions.

SmartWaySM **Excellence Award**–an annual award given by the Environmental Protection Agency (EPA) that recognizes organizational leadership in conserving energy and lowering greenhouse gas emissions from its transportation and freight activities.

social entrepreneurship–an entrepreneurial endeavor that focuses on sustainable social change, rather than merely the generation of profit.

social responsibility–*see corporate social responsibility.*

social return on investment (SROI)–a monetary measure of the social value for a community or society yielded by a specific investment.

social standards–*see standards.*

socially responsible investing (SRI)–an investment practice that gives preference to companies that value social and environmental impacts in addition to financial gain; socially responsible investments, also known as *ethical investments*, involve companies and practices that cause little or no depletion of natural assets or environmental degradation, and that do not infringe the rights of workers, women, indigenous people, children, or animals.

stakeholder engagement–the ongoing process of soliciting feedback regarding a company's business practices or major decisions from financial shareholders, as well as individuals or groups affected by corporate environmental or social practices such as suppliers, consumers, employees, and the local community.

stakeholder–an individual or group potentially affected by the activities of a company or organization; in sustainable business models the term includes financial shareholders as well as those affected by environmental or social factors such as suppliers, consumers, employees, the local community, and the natural environment.

standards–government or privately-created lists of social and environmental criteria used to regulate or evaluate the corporate responsibility of various companies; examples include the Global Reporting Initiative and UN

Global Compact as well as indexes used by socially responsible investment firms such as CERES, Calvert, and Domini.

strategic philanthropy–a corporate philanthropy or community giving program that maximizes positive impact in the community as well as for the company, including bolstered employee recruitment, retention, and a stronger company brand.

supply-side economics–the use of policies such as tax cuts and business incentives to control the supply of certain goods or services.

sustainability–the successful meeting of present social, economic, and environmental needs without compromising the ability of future generation to meet their own needs; *derived from the most common definition of sustainability, created in 1987 at the World Commission on Environment and Development.*

sustainability index–the measure of overall progress toward environmental sustainability.

sustainable design–a process of product, service, or organizational design that complies with the principles of social, economic, and environmental sustainability.

sustainable development–development that utilizes tools, supplies, and strategies that protect and enhance the earth's natural resources and diverse eco-systems so as to meet the social and economic needs of the present without compromising the ability to meet the needs of the future.

sustainable energy–energy produced both from renewable resources or by use of clean production technology.

tragedy of the commons–the inherent conflict between individual interests and the common good, based on the assumption that an individual uses a public good without considering the impact of his or her use on the availability of that good, therefore resulting in the over-exploitation of a public resource; the concept is explored in a 1968 essay written by Garrett Hardin.

transmaterialization–the process of substituting a service for a product in order to meet customer needs while reducing the use of materials and natural resources.

transparency–a measure of increased accountability and decreased corruption in which a business reports on its ethics and performance results through accessible publication of the business' practices and behavior; there is a strong movement to increase the transparency of business processes via independently-verified corporate responsibility reporting.

triple bottom line–an expansion of the traditional company reporting framework of net financial gains or losses to take into account environmental and social performance; *see people, planet, profit.*

triple top line–a phrase describing a company's improved top-line financial performance over the long term due to sustainable business practices, including less capital investment and increased revenues.

United Nations Global Compact–an international initiative that seeks to bring businesses together voluntarily in order to promote socially and environmentally responsible practices; signatories pledge to uphold the Compact's 10 Principles.

United States Business Council on Sustainable Development (USBCSD)–a non-profit organization promoting sustainable development by establishing networks and partnerships between American companies and government entities; the USBCSD provides a voice for industry and is the U.S. branch of the World Business Council of Sustainable Development.

venture philanthropy–a charitable giving model that bridges venture capital strategies with philanthropic giving, creating strategic relationships among individuals and nonprofit organizations.

waste-to-energy–a recovery process in which waste is incinerated or otherwise turned into steam or electricity, and used to generate heat, light, or power through the process of combustion.

waste-to-profit–the process of using one company's waste or by-product as the input or raw material for another company, thereby increasing business profits and decreasing waste; also referred to as byproduct synergy.

World Business Council on Sustainable Development (WBCSD)–an association of 170 international companies that provides business leadership with support to operate, innovate, and grow through sustainable development initiatives that incorporate the *three pillars of economic growth*: environmental protection, social development, and economic growth.

World Commission on Environment and Development (WCED)–*see Brundtland Commission.*

World Economic Forum–a non-profit foundation based in Geneva best known for its annual meeting in Davos, Switzerland, which brings together top business leaders, international political leaders, selected intellectuals, and journalists to discuss the most pressing issues facing the world including health and the environment. The Forum was founded by its 1000 member companies with the typical member company being a global enterprise with more than five billion dollars in turnover that is represented by various industries and regions worldwide. The Global 100 most sustainable corporations in the world are recognized annually at the Forum in Davos.

zero waste–a production system aiming to eliminate the volume and toxicity of waste and materials by conserving or recovering all resources.

Reference List for Added Reading

Aaltonen, Tapio, and Kari Tuominen (2008). *Corporate Social Responsibility Excellence Criteria : 45 Probing Questions and Contrasting Pairs of Examples*. Turku, Finland: Benchmarking Ltd. (distributed in U.S. by ASQ Quality Press Publications).

Anderson, Dan R. (2005). *Corporate Survival: The Critical Importance of Sustainability Risk Management*. Lincoln, NE: iuniverse.

Blackburn, William R. (2007). *The Sustainability Handbook*. Washington, D.C.: Island Press.

Brady, Arlo Kristjan O. (2006). *The Sustainability Effect: Rethinking Corporate Reputation in the 21st Century*. New York: Palgrave Macmillan.

Epstein, Marc J., John Elkington, Herman B. Leonard (2008). *Making Sustainability Work: Best Practices in Managing and Measuring Corporate Social, Environmental, and Economic Impacts (Business)*. Sheffield, UK: Greenleaf Publishing Limited.

Ehrenfeld, John R. (2008). *Sustainability by Design: A Subversive Strategy for Transforming Our Consumer Culture*. New Haven: Yale University Press.

Etsy, Daniel C. and Andrew S. Winston (2006). *Green to Gold*. New Haven and London: Yale University Press.

Fullan, Michael (2004). *Leadership and Sustainability: Systems Thinkers in Action*. Thousand Oaks, CA: Corwin Press.

Hawkins, David E. (2006). *Corporate Social Responsibility: Balancing Tomorrow's Sustainability and Today's Profitability*. New York: Palgrave Macmillan.

Roome, Nigel (1998). *Sustainability Strategies for Industry: The Future of Corporate Practice* (The Greening of Industry Network Series). Washington, D.C.: Island Press.

Wever, Grace (1996). *Strategic Environmental Management: Using TQEM and ISO 14000 for Competitive Advantage*. San Francisco, CA: John Wiley and Sons.

How to order or download current copies of the Baldrige Criteria for Performance Excellence:

Criteria for Performance Excellence
Baldrige National Quality Program
National Institute of Standards and Technology
Administration Building, Room A600
100 Bureau Drive, Stop 1020
Gaithersburg, MD 20899-1020
E-mail: nqp@nist.gov
Web address: http://www.quality.nist.gov

Notes

1. 2005 Environmental Sustainability Index (Benchmarking National Environmental Stewardship). Yale Center for Environmental Law and Policy. Yale University and Center for International Earth Science Information Network. Columbia University.

2. Environmental and Social Sustainability. The World Bank Group website. February 2009.

3. Corporate Sustainability Reporting. Conceptual Issues. The Corporate Sustainability Report. September 9, 2008.

4. Corporate Sustainability that Makes Business Sense. Ecostrategy Group Sustainability Strategy. 2007-2008.

5. The Business Benefits of "Going Green". Karen "KJ" Janowski. Sustainable Business. September 7, 2008.

6. Dow Jones Sustainability Indexes. Guide to Dow Jones Sustainability World Indexes. Co-published by Sustainable Asset Management (SAM). 2006.

7. NIST, Baldrige National Quality Program Criteria for Performance Excellence. Gaithersburg, MD: National Institute of Standards and Technology.

8. NIST, Baldrige National Quality Program Criteria for Performance Excellence. Gaithersburg, MD: National Institute of Standards and Technology.

9. NIST, Baldrige National Quality Program Criteria for Performance Excellence. Gaithersburg, MD: National Institute of Standards and Technology.

10. NIST, Baldrige National Quality Program Criteria for Performance Excellence. Gaithersburg, MD: National Institute of Standards and Technology.

11. Leadership Category 1 has been rewritten and revised for an organizational assessment of corporate sustainability and simplified based on Baldrige National Quality Program Criteria for Performance Excellence.

12. Strategic Planning Category 2 has been rewritten and revised for an organizational assessment of corporate sustainability and simplified based on Baldrige National Quality Program Criteria for Performance Excellence.

13. Customer Focus Category 3 has been rewritten and revised for an organizational assessment of corporate sustainability and simplified based on Baldrige National Quality Program Criteria for Performance Excellence.

14. Measurement, Analysis, and Knowledge Management Category 4 has been rewritten and revised for an organizational assessment of corporate sustainability and simplified based on Baldrige National Quality Program Criteria for Performance Excellence.

15. Workforce Focus Category 5 has been rewritten and revised for an organizational assessment of corporate sustainability and simplified based on Baldrige National Quality Program Criteria for Performance Excellence.

16. Process Management Category 6 has been rewritten and revised for an organizational assessment of corporate sustainability and simplified based on Baldrige National Quality Program Criteria for Performance Excellence.

17. Results Category 7 has been rewritten and revised for an organizational assessment of corporate sustainability and simplified based on Baldrige National Quality Program Criteria for Performance Excellence.

18. Global Reporting Initiative (GRI) framework was used as a model to develop the Baldrige Corporate Sustainability Index (BCSI).

19. NIST, Baldrige National Quality Program Criteria for Performance Excellence. Gaithersburg, MD: National Institute of Standards and Technology.

20. Dictionary of Corporate Responsibility & Sustainability Terms. Brownflynn. http://www.brownflynn.com/RESOURCECENTER/glossary.

21. Global Reporting Initiative © 2006 www.globalreporting.org. Reprinted with permission.

22. Global Reporting Initiative © 2006 www.globalreporting.org. Reprinted with permission.

23. Global Reporting Initiative © 2006 www.globalreporting.org. Reprinted with permission.

Index

About the Author

Donald C. Fisher, Ph.D.

Donald Fisher, Executive Director/CEO of Mid-South Quality Productivity Center—The Quality Center (a partnership between the Greater Memphis Chamber and Southwest Tennessee Community College) in Memphis, Tennessee, a Tennessee Board of Regents Center of Quality Emphasis, has presented the Malcolm Baldrige Award Criteria internationally to Hitachi, Ltd. in Japan, to the Center for Productivity in Maracaibo, Venezuela, and to a group of international suppliers in London. He has also consulted with officials from the Venezuelan Ministry of Development who have reviewed adopting the Malcolm Baldrige Criteria as a model for their National Quality Award. He has worked as a visiting scholar (Commissioned by the World Bank) with the President and Prime Minister of Mauritius (an island nation located in the Indian Ocean) to oversee that nation's first ever Baldrige award program. In addition, he worked with the Federal Express Corporation in Dubai, United Arab Emirates, on their Baldrige Application for the Dubai Quality Award. He has worked with 85 presidents of worldwide companies owned by the Hong Leong management group in Kuala Lumpur, Malaysia to help them use Baldrige criteria for strategic planning. Fisher also served as an advisor for Gate Gourmet International (a division of SwissAir) "Global Service Excellence" Baldrige project in Zurich, Switzerland. Fisher is a multi-year veteran of the Board of Examiners for the prestigious Malcolm Baldrige National Quality Award and has judged quality performance based on the Baldrige criteria for more than 170 leading organizations worldwide. He has traveled throughout the world helping organizations with awards similar to the Baldrige Award. He is the author or co-author of a number of books, including *The Simplified Baldrige Award Organization Assessment, Demystifying Baldrige, Measuring Up to the Baldrige, Baldrige on Campus, The Baldrige Workbook for Healthcare,* and *Homeland Security Assessment Manual (A Comprehensive Organizational Assessment Based on Baldrige Criteria).* In addition, he serves on numerous quality boards throughout the United States and the world.

He presently serves on the Board of Director's of the Alliance for Performance Excellence, the organization that oversees all the Baldrige-based state and local Awards throughout the United States. In addition he serves as a judge for the Arizona State Quality Award and was a founding member of the board of directors and one of seven Quality Award judges for the Tennessee Center for Performance Excellence (TNCPE). He is a past member of the Advisory Board and presently serves on Panel of Judges for the Commonwealth of Kentucky Quality Award and has served as both a director and judge for the Greater Memphis Award for Quality. In addition to these appointments, he was appointed to serve on both the President's Quality Award Program Panel of Judges in Washington D.C. and was selected as one of eight senior judges for the Secretary of the Air Force Unit Quality Award. He served as a consultant to the National Association of College and University Business Officers (NACUBO) National Project on developing its Baldrige-based Management Achievement Award (MAA) for American colleges and universities. In addition he served seven years as a judge for the RIT/USA Today Quality Cup Team Award.

Fisher's credentials for writing this book include spending over 20 years using Baldrige Criteria to conduct organizational assessments of various global organizations such as FedEx Corporation, Volvo-GM Heavy Truck Corporation, Cargill Corn Milling North America, Bama Companies, Hong Leong Corporation Malaysia, and St. Jude Children's Research Hospital.

His extensive research, along with his early involvement as a Baldrige examiner, give Fisher unique knowledge and credentials related to corporate sustainability planning and the use of the Baldrige Criteria as a corporate sustainability assessment tool.

Fisher has developed a corporate sustainability training system entitled Process Activated Training System® (PATS), which is used by the United States Postal Service nationwide. This system has been used to transform best practice sustainability initiatives into training scripts. Learn more about PATS at www.Processactivatedtraining .com.

Belong to the Quality Community!

Established in 1946, ASQ is a global community of quality experts in all fields and industries. ASQ is dedicated to the promotion and advancement of quality tools, principles, and practices in the workplace and in the community.

The Society also serves as an advocate for quality. Its members have informed and advised the U.S. Congress, government agencies, state legislatures, and other groups and individuals worldwide on quality-related topics.

Vision

By making quality a global priority, an organizational imperative, and a personal ethic, ASQ becomes the community of choice for everyone who seeks quality technology, concepts, or tools to improve themselves and their world.

ASQ is...

- More than 90,000 individuals and 700 companies in more than 100 countries

- The world's largest organization dedicated to promoting quality

- A community of professionals striving to bring quality to their work and their lives

- The administrator of the Malcolm Baldrige National Quality Award

- A supporter of quality in all sectors including manufacturing, service, healthcare, government, and education

- YOU

Visit www.asq.org for more information.

ASQ Membership

Research shows that people who join associations experience increased job satisfaction, earn more, and are generally happier*. ASQ membership can help you achieve this while providing the tools you need to be successful in your industry and to distinguish yourself from your competition. So why wouldn't you want to be a part of ASQ?

Networking

Have the opportunity to meet, communicate, and collaborate with your peers within the quality community through conferences and local ASQ section meetings, ASQ forums or divisions, ASQ Communities of Quality discussion boards, and more.

Professional Development

Access a wide variety of professional development tools such as books, training, and certifications at a discounted price. Also, ASQ certifications and the ASQ Career Center help enhance your quality knowledge and take your career to the next level.

Solutions

Find answers to all your quality problems, big and small, with ASQ's Knowledge Center, mentoring program, various e-newsletters, *Quality Progress* magazine, and industry-specific products.

Access to Information

Learn classic and current quality principles and theories in ASQ's Quality Information Center (QIC), *ASQ Weekly* e-newsletter, and product offerings.

Advocacy Programs

ASQ helps create a better community, government, and world through initiatives that include social responsibility, Washington advocacy, and Community Good Works.

Visit www.asq.org/membership for more information on ASQ membership.

*2008, The William E. Smith Institute for Association Research

ASQ Certification

ASQ certification is formal recognition by ASQ that an individual has demonstrated a proficiency within, and comprehension of, a specified body of knowledge at a point in time. Nearly 150,000 certifications have been issued. ASQ has members in more than 100 countries, in all industries, and in all cultures. ASQ certification is internationally accepted and recognized.

Benefits to the Individual

- New skills gained and proficiency upgraded
- Investment in your career
- Mark of technical excellence
- Assurance that you are current with emerging technologies
- Discriminator in the marketplace
- Certified professionals earn more than their uncertified counterparts
- Certification is endorsed by more than 125 companies

Benefits to the Organization

- Investment in the company's future
- Certified individuals can perfect and share new techniques in the workplace
- Certified staff are knowledgeable and able to assure product and service quality

Quality is a global concept. It spans borders, cultures, and languages. No matter what country your customers live in or what language they speak, they demand quality products and services. You and your organization also benefit from quality tools and practices. Acquire the knowledge to position yourself and your organization ahead of your competition.

Certifications Include

- Biomedical Auditor – CBA
- Calibration Technician – CCT
- HACCP Auditor – CHA
- Pharmaceutical GMP Professional – CPGP
- Quality Inspector – CQI
- Quality Auditor – CQA
- Quality Engineer – CQE
- Quality Improvement Associate – CQIA
- Quality Technician – CQT
- Quality Process Analyst – CQPA
- Reliability Engineer – CRE
- Six Sigma Black Belt – CSSBB
- Six Sigma Green Belt – CSSGB
- Software Quality Engineer – CSQE
- Manager of Quality/Organizational Excellence – CMQ/OE

Visit www.asq.org/certification to apply today!

ASQ Training

Classroom-based Training

ASQ offers training in a traditional classroom setting on a variety of topics. Our instructors are quality experts and lead courses that range from one day to four weeks, in several different cities. Classroom-based training is designed to improve quality and your organization's bottom line. Benefit from quality experts; from comprehensive, cutting-edge information; and from peers eager to share their experiences.

Web-based Training

Virtual Courses

ASQ's virtual courses provide the same expert instructors, course materials, interaction with other students, and ability to earn CEUs and RUs as our classroom-based training, without the hassle and expenses of travel. Learn in the comfort of your own home or workplace. All you need is a computer with Internet access and a telephone.

Self-paced Online Programs

These online programs allow you to work at your own pace while obtaining the quality knowledge you need. Access them whenever it is convenient for you, accommodating your schedule.

Some Training Topics Include

- Auditing
- Basic Quality
- Engineering
- Education
- Healthcare
- Government
- Food Safety
- ISO
- Leadership
- Lean
- Quality Management
- Reliability
- Six Sigma
- Social Responsibility

Visit www.asq.org/training for more information.